T0197206

A Quest for the *Golden Pond:*

A Mother's Spiritual Journey While Caring for her Sick Son

KATE RICHARDSON

BALBOA.PRESS
A DIVISION OF HAY HOUSE

Copyright © 2020 Kate Richardson.

All rights reserved. No part of this book may be used or reproduced by
any means, graphic, electronic, or mechanical, including photocopying,
recording, taping or by any information storage retrieval system
without the written permission of the author except in the case
of brief quotations embodied in critical articles and reviews.

Balboa Press books may be ordered through booksellers or by contacting:

Balboa Press
A Division of Hay House
1663 Liberty Drive
Bloomington, IN 47403
www.balboapress.com
1 (877) 407-4847

Because of the dynamic nature of the Internet, any web addresses or
links contained in this book may have changed since publication and
may no longer be valid. The views expressed in this work are solely those
of the author and do not necessarily reflect the views of the publisher,
and the publisher hereby disclaims any responsibility for them.

The author of this book does not dispense medical advice or prescribe the use
of any technique as a form of treatment for physical, emotional, or medical
problems without the advice of a physician, either directly or indirectly. The
intent of the author is only to offer information of a general nature to help
you in your quest for emotional and spiritual well-being. In the event you use
any of the information in this book for yourself, which is your constitutional
right, the author and the publisher assume no responsibility for your actions.

Any people depicted in stock imagery provided by Getty Images are
models, and such images are being used for illustrative purposes only.
Certain stock imagery © Getty Images.

Print information available on the last page.

ISBN: 978-1-9822-4621-1 (sc)
ISBN: 978-1-9822-4622-8 (e)

Balboa Press rev. date: 05/18/2020

CONTENTS

CONTENTS

Why I wrote a book even though I am afraid someone might read it.

In May 2015, my son was diagnosed with cancer which sent me plummeting down a rabbit hole with unfathomable depths. This trauma resulted in a spiritual journey in order to survive the event and move towards healing. I have always used writing as a tool in order to organize my thoughts and ideas. This includes journaling in order to sort out my feelings and uncover areas where I need improvement.

When my son was diagnosed with cancer, I opened a Facebook page in order to inform everyone about Jack's progress during treatment. The Facebook page became my forum for healing through writing. I wrote several posts (not only updating everyone on Jack's progress) but sharing my thoughts and feelings as I moved through the process as well. This book is a collection of some of those Facebook posts along with me expounding on some of these ideas in the text.

My writing was a methodology for healing my severely injured soul. It was not easy to share my soul self with others (it was much like sharing a diary), but it was an important part of the process in order to assist the healing within myself. I wrote this book with the same idea in mind. I wrote it as a methodology for me to organize my thoughts and feelings; therefore, furthering and deepening the healing which needed to take place.

As I was writing the book, I began to understand the

importance of all human beings sharing their stories and miracles with one another. We are all Teachers and we are all Students. We can learn from one another. I began to realize that if I could find the courage to share my story and ideas with others, it may help others on their path to healing. Even if it is helpful for one or two people, then it was worth writing.

So, I decided to set my fears of judgment and vulnerability aside and move towards having this book published. Even if you do not agree with my thoughts and perceptions on healing, it may open a door within yourself to consider your own thoughts and perceptions on the topic. If this book pushes you to look within, then I consider it a success.

Thank you for your open-mindedness. Thank you for being the Teacher and the Student. Thank you for choosing to read my story. I hope it gives you the courage to share your story and miracles with the outside world as well.

CHAPTER 1

The Beginning of
Tumultuous Change

*W*here does the healing start when someone goes through something traumatic? There are natural ups and downs in life that everyone experiences, but what do you do when you are challenged with something larger? Something you feel like you do not have the capacity to handle. When the carpet has been pulled beneath your feet and you hit the earth hard, you wonder how you never knew the ground was so unforgiving. We all have this journey we call life, and although our journeys are different, we are all trying to arrive at the same place. A place of peace, calm, and tranquility. A place where you realize the tension in your shoulders that kept them stiff and connected to your earlobes was never a necessary thing to experience. When you go through a traumatic experience, you wonder if such a place even exists, and if it will ever be possible for you to reach it. You may feel like you are experiencing a hell on earth that no one can respond or relate to. You may feel so separate from the rest of the population, that it is difficult to believe that you could possibly be on the same path as everyone else. But you are. And you can move through these seemingly impossible experiences to make you stronger.

This trauma has a momentum which will awaken your senses and move your state of mind into a new perspective that will drive you to that place of peacefulness sooner rather than later.

And, although the paths we take may vary, the end result does not. We are never alone. Although our paths may diverge, we are still on the same journey together. Touching people along the way and building them to their ultimate potential. Yet, when something traumatic happens, the wind is knocked out of your lungs initially, and you wonder if the breath you desperately need to live will ever enter your lungs again. You take in big gulps of air in hopes that it will somehow heal you or change the situation. If only you could *breathe*. These are some of the realizations I came to when my son was diagnosed with cancer. This was a terrible situation where I was fortunate to have been able to transmute the pain, sadness, and depression that surrounded his diagnosis and cancer treatment to a journey towards inner peace and healing. This is my journey, but you are all along with me for the ride. Please join me on my walk to something more beautiful. Let's learn to heal together.

I used to pray every night before I went to bed. I always believed in a God or Higher Power, although I couldn't understand him. Why do you allow your children to suffer? No one deserves pain, so why would you bring it upon them? My prayers were always very much the same. I always tried to bargain with God. I would ask him that if the duality of the Universe insisted that bad things had to happen to someone, that it would happen to me only. I asked God to leave my children unscathed. To wrap them in his power of peace and love and keep them whole and safe. Needless to say, when my son was diagnosed with cancer, I immediately was angry with God. I wished it was me who had to suffer the nauseating chemotherapy and mood swings of the steroids. I wished it was me who had to be hospitalized and kept from my friends due to a suppressed immune system. It was difficult for me to bring any semblance of acceptance to my life situation. But all stories have a beginning, so let me introduce you to (what I felt like at the time) was the beginning of the end of my life.

My son, Jack, was in the third grade. He enjoyed playing video games and attending Tae Kwon Do classes. He was living a very normal life for an eight-year-old. It all began with pain in his right leg. As parents, we assumed he pulled a muscle in Tae Kwon Do, told him to rest it, and gave him Tylenol. All the normal things a parent does when their kid becomes injured. Then, one day in March 2015, he was riding in the car with his Dad and sister. He told them his bottom felt weird. He said it didn't hurt, but just felt "weird." He described it as uncomfortable. We took him to the doctor. The doctor told us he was fine. We went to Mexico over Spring break. On the plane ride to Mexico, he cried the whole time because of the "weird" feeling on his bottom and leg pain. Once we arrived in Mexico, he limped for most of the trip. This pain in the leg and bottom occurred on and off for some time. There were intermittent doctor visits where they kept telling us there was nothing wrong with him. We knew deep in our hearts that something was wrong, and we were confused on the best course of action to take next. Then, the pain became so great that we drove him to the emergency room. The emergency room doctor said he would do a CT scan of the area, although he didn't expect to find anything.

After the CT scan, the doctor asked me to walk into the hallway. He told me there was a tumor in my son's pelvic area, and a section of it was wrapped around (but not quite touching) his spinal cord. My stomach dropped. I was in shock. You read about this happening to other people, but somehow think that you are immune to it. My body went numb. I was talking to the doctor, but I felt like I wasn't present in my body. I could hear my voice responding to the doctor's words, but it sounded far away. I tried not to start crying, afraid that the tears might frighten my son. The pain/weird feeling he was having in his pelvic region was due to this tumor. The tumor was pressing on nerves in his pelvis (which explained the weird feeling in his bottom), and it was pushing on his sciatic nerve (which was the cause of all his

3

leg pain). It can be more adequately summed up in the Facebook post I made to inform friends and loved ones of our unexpected tragedy.

> Well, it has been an emotional roller coaster since Monday. I (Jack's mom) have set up this FB account in order to more easily give updates on how Jack's diagnosis/treatment is progressing.
>
> I would like to thank everyone for their support so far. It has been a trying time, but it has really lifted us up as a family to see the support from our friends and family.
>
> Last week, Jack saw his pediatrician for pain in his groin area and left knee. The pain was not constant, but it became more severe throughout the week. The first set of lab work done by his pediatrician came back normal. By Monday morning, Jack was crying and screaming in pain, so my husband and I took him to the emergency room at Provena Hospital in Urbana, Illinois. They did a CT scan of Jack's body and located a 6-7 cm mass in his pelvic region with the largest portion of the mass on the left side. The mass also appeared to be wrapped around his spine. Jack was sent by ambulance from Provena to The Children's Hospital of Illinois located at OSF Hospital in Peoria, Illinois.
>
> When my husband and I first spoke to the oncologist, she was pretty certain the symptoms and where the mass was located were signs of either sarcoma or neuroblastoma. These are solid tumors which would affect a person for the rest of their lives with a 50% chance of survival.

Best treatment for this would be at St. Jude's Hospital in Memphis, Tennessee.

On Wednesday, the pediatric surgical/oncology team conducted a biopsy of the tumor in Jack's pelvis. This was a surgical procedure. On Thursday morning, Jack's oncologist had good news for us. The tumor was not consistent with sarcoma or neuroblastoma. Instead, it was more consistent with lymphoma or leukemia.

This was good news because lymphoma and leukemia have more successful survival rates, and they are more treatable than sarcoma or neuroblastoma. On Thursday, at 3:00 pm, Jack's medical team placed a port in his chest and took bone marrow samples from Jack. This was Jack's second surgical procedure. The bone marrow samples will tell us if Jack's diagnosis will be lymphoma or leukemia. We are expecting results later today. The port in his chest is where Jack will receive his chemotherapy treatments. They will be able to take blood work from this port also which means less needle pricks for Jack. Jack received the type of port that can be submerged in water. This is more good news because he will be able to take baths and swim. The port he would have received for the other diagnosis would not have allowed this.

Jack woke up from his surgical sleep at 1:00 am this morning yelling, "Mom, wake up, I'm hungry." He chowed on teddy grahams and potato chips, and he was in no pain from the second procedure.

We have many hurdles ahead, but I feel blessed that Jack's diagnosis is looking better than it did initially. And I feel blessed that so many friends and family have given us prayers and support. Jack especially loved that everyone was writing "JACK" on their hands to remember to think and pray for him during this difficult time.

Jack's attitude has been positive throughout (although he gets the most angry when his doctors won't let him eat prior to surgeries). With all the love and support we have received, I'm sure he will be able to maintain that positive attitude.

I will post more as I receive more information. Thanks and love to you all for your thoughts, prayers, and support. It has already made a huge impact in our lives, and it will not be forgotten. -Facebook post dated May 2015

CHAPTER 2

Being Presented with a Choice

On the ambulance ride to a nearby hospital, where the closest children's oncology unit resided, several nightmarish thoughts were wreaking havoc on my mind. Although I didn't realize it at the time, I was being presented with a choice. Not a choice in the conventional sense, where I could choose whether or not my son had cancer, but I had a choice on how to react to and perceive the present situation. To be positive or negative. To be brave or cry all the way to the hospital. I would love to tell you I was brave, accepted my situation, and was the picture of strength my son needed at the time. But that would be a lie. My mind went through the cycling downward spiral of possible negative outcomes, anxiety, and fear. I thought I would never have control over my life or feel any type of happiness again. Sometimes the way we react to a negative situation will dictate the energy and possible outcomes that could assist the situation. When a person can find the calm center or inner peace, then they are usually able to make better decisions; therefore, having better possible outcomes to the negative situation. A story to illustrate. The Dragon or the Light.

> Once upon a time, there were twin princesses who lived in a kingdom far away. The twin girls had everything they desired. Expensive clothing, a palace as their home, kind parents, servants, and a multitude of friends for companionship. However, the twin princesses felt like something

was missing from their lives. There was almost a boredom or ennui behind everything they did. They were often anxious because they felt as though they should be happy, but that feeling of "not-quite-rightness" acted as a barrier against their happiness. One day, they asked their friends to create new games to play. The new games were fun and distracted the twins from the emptiness for some time, but the "something is missing" feeling returned. They learned new languages, learned martial arts, learned how to hunt with a bow, learned how to sew and stitch clothes, and learned to cook and bake. The list of ideas they found to fill the hole of emptiness was unlimited. And each hobby seemed to distract them for a little while, and they thought that listless, anxious feeling was gone. Yet, after conquering each new endeavor, the "something is missing" feeling would return even more hungry than before.

Months rolled by, and there came a time when their happy kingdom was at war. The twin's father, the King, met his adversaries on the battle lines. The war and constant battles continued for three months. The twin princesses busied themselves with tending to, healing, and feeding the wounded soldiers. They felt happy to assist in any way. And, this distracted them for a little while, and they thought this might have been what was missing to help them feel complete. On the final day of battle, the kingdom won, but it was at a cost. The King was slain. The twin princesses wailed with grief over the death of their father. Their mother loved the King very much, and she died of a broken heart two weeks later. Now, the twin princesses felt even more empty inside. They could no longer gaze upon the walls of their home without feeling a deep sense of loss over their parent's death. Their older brother took over as ruler of the kingdom. Although, the twin princesses wanted to assist him in ruling the kingdom, a deep sadness consumed them. The walls of the palace acted as a reminder of their parent's deaths and the familial closeness they had lost.

With heavy hearts, the twin princesses waited until it was dark one night, and they left the palace. They wandered in the woods for days, scavenging food, and sleeping on the cool earth at night. Something about sleeping on the ground gave them peace, but when they would awaken, they were only reminded of the reality of their parent's deaths and what seemed like their never-ending grief and desolation.

One day, they stumbled upon a cave deep in the forest. They were contemplating whether or not to explore the inside of the cave, when a gnarled old woman appeared at the cave opening. The twin princesses asked the gnarled old woman if the cave was her home. The woman nodded her head and told them she had something of interest to them. The princesses weren't sure if it was a trick or kindness but decided to take the chance and enter the cave with the woman.

Once inside the cave, the old woman said, "I would like to fill the emptiness in your souls. I can tell they have been emptied for some time.

9

Your choice stands before you. Choose wisely."
The old woman motioned to the wall of the cave
where two large picture frames hung from the
rocky crag. The twin princesses approached
the two picture frames to see the images which
laid within them. One frame contained a fire-
breathing dragon with red and black shimmering
scales and powerful pointed wings. The other
frame contained nothing but a pure white,
formless, shimmering light.

The old woman said, "You can choose to
stay in your current form and wander the woods
aimlessly or you can both choose to inhabit one
of the forms in the two pictures instead. The
choice is for each of you to make."

The twin princesses thought about it and
decided they each wanted to take a different
form. They were tired of the ever-present void
in their lives and wanted to be something...
anything different. One of the princesses was
still enraged at the loss of her parents. She told
the old woman, "I choose to become the dragon.
In this form, I will smite all the people who were
responsible for my parent's death." With that,
this princess touched the picture frame which
contained the dragon, transformed into its
image, and flew swiftly out of the cave.

The other princess decided to become the
pure white light. She told the old woman, "I
choose to be the formless light. I don't know
why, but it beckons to me and whispers peaceful
things to my soul." And then, this princess
touched the picture frame which contained the
formless white light, transformed into its image,

and disappeared into a different place not of this world.

And, so it came to pass the dragon princess enacted the very revenge she sought after. She ransacked the lands of those who fought against their kingdom. She spit fire onto their homes and tore at them with her claws, so they would deteriorate even faster. But the emptiness was still there. She burnt every single one of the townspeople to a heap of blackened ashes. But the emptiness was still there. She killed all the livestock with her claws and ate their steaming carcasses. But the emptiness was still there. She killed all the plant life, the trees, and the crops. But the emptiness was still there. When the lands that opposed her kingdom were completely devoid of people and any life whatsoever, her goal had been achieved. There was nothing left to destroy. But the emptiness was still there.

The dragon princess was saddened by the fact that her revenge had not made her complete. She knew she could not return to her kingdom in her present state, so she retreated to the nearby cave where she met the bargaining woman who gave her scales and the ability to breathe fire. The woman was no longer there; however, the cave made a suitable home for a lost dragon, so there she stayed. The dragon princess felt utterly alone, filled with more sadness than ever before, and she desperately missed her sister. Most fairy tales will tell you that a fierce dragon cannot cry, but this is not the truth. The dragon princess cried bitterly with salty dragon tears running down her face until they reached her mouth where they were dried quickly by her fiery hot breath. The dragon princess remained in this state for many days.

When the other princess chose the light picture, she was immediately transported to a formless world full of pure white light. Her own transformational light moved through and was connected to all the other wisps of light in this world. She had never felt more at peace or more complete. She was constantly full of happiness, joy, and peace. There was no sadness or pain in this world. Instead, there was a constant stream of joyful contentment. This positive existence was hard to describe with words, but she felt true freedom for the first time in her life. The happiness rolled over her, through her, and into everything else that was a part of this world. The peaceful feeling was magnified by the same peaceful feelings of the other light beings around her. She was one with everything. The power behind this oneness caused a tingling, static electricity-type feeling throughout her entire being and reverberated throughout her new consciousness.

The light princess paused and heard a faint faraway cry. She knew the sounds of anguish came from her former world, and she wanted to heal the pain this creature was experiencing. The light princess returned to her past world in her light form and followed the tormented cries to the cave where she met the old woman. She floated and moved through the cave until she met her sister, the dragon. The dragon princess was afraid when she witnessed the light. She growled and threw fire at the formless being. Then, the dragon princess heard a voice. It was a voice she remembered from long ago. It was her sister.

"Why do you cry?" the light princess asked.

"Dear sister, I have vanquished our parent's enemies. Not a house, not a structure, not an animal, person, or plant remain on those lands. Only the ashes that I turned them into. I should feel avenged and complete, but I feel even more empty than before," the dragon princess answered.

"Perhaps, you are tired of the dragon, and ready for a greater truth?" the light princess asked.

"Yes, I am tired of being a dragon, but the thought of returning to human form is even more upsetting. I should have been wise like you and chosen the light form," the dragon sister replied.

"Who says it is too late to choose? Reach your claw out to me and return to your true home," beckoned the light princess.

"But the old woman said we only had one choice. She said the choice could not be changed or redeemed. I am stuck in this form forever," the dragon princess sulked.

"The old woman would have you believe this because she cannot exist without your pain, but I know better. Trust me, dear sister. Reach out to me and I will guide you home," said the light princess.

The dragon sister could feel the peace and joy emanating from her sister's new form and it called to her. The dragon sister reached out to her sister's new form. Upon touching her sister's light form, the scales and claws disappeared as though they never appeared in the first place. The features of the dragon dissipated like a fog lifting to expose the features of a new world. The dragon sister looked down and happily saw she had taken on the same form as her sister. Delighted at the transformation, the former dragon princess finally felt the emptiness lift. She felt united with everything just like her sister. The wholeness and truth filled her entire being with peace and love. They were one and together for all eternity. They returned to their true home of serene beauty and complete companionship. They returned to a place they had forgotten in their worldly form but had always belonged to in reality.

The truth emanating from this story is also applicable to our everyday lives. There is a natural occurrence of ups and downs throughout a person's lifetime. The two princesses began their life in a seemingly paradisiacal palace. They had loving parents, money, and friends. All their bodily needs were met. These things eventually dissolved when a war took away their parents. Where they felt listless and bored in the castle before, now they felt as though the proverbial rug had been pulled from under their feet. Everything they identified as their truth (along with its foundation) was shattered.

Sometimes when the truth (which we have built around ourselves) has been obliterated, we panic. We don't know what action to take. Our minds quickly go through an endless stream of possible solutions to the problem, but none of these solutions seem to have the resolution. We may search desperately for the comforts of our palace only to find there never was a palace. This is the reason the princesses felt as though something was missing long before the war took their parents. The world they knew was built upon a false truth of separation. What was missing all along was the **real** truth which was hidden deep within themselves. The Light of God. Enlightenment. A oneness with ascended masters. Union with Mother Earth and the Universe. Whatever title or concept gives you the most comfort is fine. They are all different words for the same truth.

When we forget our true identity and lose our way on our life's journey, we feel disconnected from our Source. Again, this concept of "Source" can be called anything that gives you peace (God, Atman, Buddha, etc). For the purposes of this book, I will use several different terms to describe the same concept of Source. I understand different people will have positive or negative reactions to certain spiritual words or phrases; therefore, I think it is important to use many different words for the same truth (which I believe all have the same meaning).

The princesses felt uneasy (even before the war) because they had forgotten their true selves. They had lost touch with the connection of their Source. Our true being is one of infinite light and togetherness. It is easy to forget this truth while we are inhabiting separate bodies on Earth and we become blind to the light that connects all things. Our Source is where we originated (I.E. the light form in the story). This light connects all things. When we fail to remember that this light is within everything, then we become disturbed or upset. We feel as though we are separated from our Source, and this creates pain which can present itself in many physical forms in this life.

Even though the princesses seemingly had everything at the beginning of the story, they still felt as though something was missing. The missing part of their lives was remembering the oneness of all things in conjunction with their original Source. Being in human form (instead of their original spirit form) had caused them to forget their Source. Since they were unable to identify what was missing from their lives when things were comfortable, it became even more difficult for them when things began going "wrong." After the war, the palace only reminded them of their past, and they were no longer comfortable in the protective walls of the castle. While continuing to live within these walls, the princesses were stuck in a pain cycle created by the constant memories of their past. They thought the palace and their parents would always be their protective refuge. When this disappeared, the pain and feelings of unsafety became their prominent new reality. In order to attempt to escape these feelings, they ventured out into the world.

Something particularly important here to note. Humanity, in general, needs to learn to let go of the fear of pain. Sometimes, painful experiences in our lives can be a catalyst for massive, positive change on our lifepaths. It can completely alter our perceptions and make manifest needed change and growth in our lives. The pain the princesses experienced gave them two options: to stay in the home marked with pain (and continue living unhappily in the past) or to recognize the need for transformation (and venture on a new pathway) in hopes of healing. The princesses encountered this painful experience which forced them to make a conscious decision regarding the discomfort they had been feeling deep within their souls all along. Although, they were uncertain of the new path laid before them, they were no longer content with the manufactured walls and false state of being contained in their former home. This pain caused them to embark on a journey that would ultimately assist them in finding their Source and true form. This tragedy was necessary for positive spiritual transformation in the princess's lives.

When the princesses came upon the witch in the forest, they were desperate for any guidance whatsoever. The witch represented the ego in all of us (or the representation of wanting to be individual, separate, special, and apart from everything else). However, the witch's presentation of the formless light gave the princesses the option of a truth that they did not remember. Therefore, the witch acted as a necessary guide for them on their life journey. The witch insinuated there was only one permanent choice to be made. The ego wants you to think past choices cannot be redeemed. This is not true. You can choose the light at any time no matter what decisions you have made in the past. The truth is always waiting to greet you with open arms.

You may think the princesses never would have been united with their true selves had they not met with the witch. This is somewhat true because the ego is a necessary part of our journey. However, the dragon princess may have united with her true self earlier had she not believed the witch's lies. The ego/witch presented the true light form as an option, but she did not think either princess would choose it. The witch attempted to reveal the formless light to scare them because she believed the princesses were both attached to bodily form. She miscalculated the depth of the light princess's wisdom when she gave that choice and the light princess chose correctly. The dragon princess was afraid of the formless white light because she was still identified with form. In addition, the dragon princess's inner voice was deafened by the ego's need for revenge, so she could not hear her truth beckoning to her when she looked at the formless white light.

At last, the choice to become something different. The princess who chose to be a dragon chose revenge as her path. This form was even further from the reality of her true self than her human body; therefore, she felt even more empty and alone as a consequence. The princess who chose to be the light form immediately remembered her true self and knew she had found the answer to the emptiness she was feeling in her body. Yet, the dragon princess's choice was not irredeemable. Again, the pain and loneliness she felt as a dragon caused her to ultimately choose the same path as her sister, which brought her to the truth and her Source. Further pain was a necessary part of her journey to be at peace.

Day to day, we are always presented with a choice. We cannot always choose what happens to us. We cannot always choose our circumstances. We cannot always choose the good and bad things that appear to happen to us in our everyday lives. However, we can ALWAYS choose how we react and how we perceive the event. We can choose to look past the pain and discomfort, and see the truth and light buried deep in everything around us. If we close our eyes, acknowledge the pain, and discern why we feel it, we have the option within us to move past this seeming obstacle. To release the pain and let it go. We have the option of watching this deeply buried light rise to the surface in all of the seemingly separate forms surrounding us. Our most upsetting problems can be transformed to light and truth.

The light buried deep within us is powerful enough to accomplish this feat. The truth and light are present no matter what appears to be taking place in our lives ("good" or "bad"). If we are vigilant, we can break the cycles of pain in our lives and move towards finding oneness with our true Source. We can never go wrong if we choose the picture frame filled with light. However, if we are in a state of mind that wants to choose the dragon, then that's okay too. Just remember to extend love and patience to yourself in this process. The light will always be waiting for you when you are ready for it.

CHAPTER 3

The Importance of Togetherness

The first week of Jack's cancer diagnosis was particularly hard for his father and me to digest. We were walking along the "carpet of life," if you will. Formerly, the carpet always stayed in place as we were walking on it. We were a normal family involved in normal family routines and activities on the "normal" course of life. Not to say we did not experience the normal ups and downs of life; however, there was nothing groundbreaking that rocked our foundation. As soon as we were informed about the tumor in our son's pelvis, this all changed. Before, we walked along the carpet of life assuredly. We did not keep our knees bent to anticipate a fall. We were complacent with the carpet and thought it would kindly guide us through life without any major hiccups. When the doctor told me there was a tumor in Jack's pelvis, the rug was pulled out from under my feet and I hit the ground. Hard. I had not been walking on the rug tentatively anticipating the sudden movement in bad fortune. I felt as though I was falling for an hour before I finally hit the floor. And, when I finally could comprehend what was being said to me, I had no idea how to adequately process the information. I felt as though my husband, my son, and I would never feel safe again.

As the week in the hospital crawled by, I became extremely dependent on the doctor's words, the nurse's kindness, and the love and support that ensued from family, friends, and the community in which we lived. I couldn't trust the now fragile state of my world, and no matter how long I lay awake on the hospital couch at night, I could not identify the answer to overcome the despair I was feeling. Initially, the doctors thought Jack had neuroblastoma or ewing sarcoma based on the location of the tumor. These type of childhood cancers are treatable, but do not have good long-term prognoses. We were coming to terms with the possibility that we were going to outlive our son, and I, particularly was handling the situation very poorly.

I was embracing the dragon in the princess story. I was trying to stay positive on the surface, but deep below an anger was welling up inside of me. I remember walking down the hallway of the hospital and peering into a room with an open door. There was a teenager sitting on the bed with a cast covering her broken leg. She and her mother were watching television together and laughing. What should have filled my heart with happiness over the positive interaction between mother and daughter, filled me with bitterness instead. "Must be nice," I thought. "You will get to spend your entire life with your daughter. My son is going to die before I do. I would do anything to trade places with you." The bitterness sickened my heart and only made things worse for me, yet I still clung to the dragon persona. As though that dark, tarry bitterness would place a barrier around my heart and prevent me from feeling any more pain.

What helped bring me through it were the positive interactions I had with other people, especially that first week. I was still clinging to the bitterness; however, the optimism that surrounded me caused some of that blackness to crack and reveal the light within. I came to the realization that we humans all need each other. And, the pleasant affirmations and the never-ending kindness people extended to us that first week made a huge difference. I could write a book as a stand-alone novel on the many ways people built us up with their uplifting spirits that week. But the below encounter is my favorite, and I think it illustrates a salient point regarding how badly humanity needs each other (and although we are all contained in separate bodies) how connected we truly are.

The first week of Jack's diagnosis, I was bombarded with phone calls, text messages, and emails because everyone wanted to know if Jack was alright. Although social media was not my favorite pastime, I decided that creating a Facebook account would be a good way to facilitate communication with everyone. Jack's upcoming cancer diagnosis and treatment had updates and new information every day, and Facebook became the mechanism for keeping loved ones and friends informed. One, this was easier on me because I only had to post one update instead of repeating the same information over and over to different people. Two, only having to post it once was healthy for me at the time, so I wouldn't have to relive the painful information I was relaying over and over again to several different people.

People were posting very kind things on Jack's Facebook page. Funny videos, positive comments, jokes, and lots and lots of love. They were extending all these positive vibes through their fingertips on their computers and smart phones to us, and they were being received by our family in a very big way. But, the one that stands out to me the most came from our family friend, John. He wrote Jack's name on his hand in permanent marker and posted a picture of it on Facebook. Underneath the picture, John posted that he wrote Jack on his hand so that he would remember to send positive thoughts Jack's way every time he looked down at it.

Soon after, several other people were following suit. We asked one of the nurses for a permanent marker in the hospital and wrote Jack on our hands. All our friends and family were writing "Jack" on their hands and posting the pictures all over Facebook. But the posts didn't stop there. Some people were posting pictures of Jack's name in the sand. Another person made a plaque with a hand painted on it with Jack's name placed neatly in the center. Then, the day before Jack's biopsy (to

21

identify what type of cancer he had) John's wife, Cheryl, posted a mass message on Facebook.

She said Jack was receiving a biopsy the next day and needed everyone's help. She explained that people in our community were writing Jack's name on their hands in order to remember to send positive thoughts and prayers to him during this difficult time. She asked the Facebook world if they would do the same. And, they did. Our Facebook page was flooded with pictures from across the entire country. People we have never met were posting pictures of Jack's name on their hand and wishing him well. The response was overwhelming and gave us much needed emotional support. It gave us something uplifting to focus on in a time which was otherwise marked only for stress and worry. Maybe if people that didn't know Jack personally were kind enough to send encouragement, then the world wasn't so bad after all. Maybe we would find a way to survive this life situation.

Again, the first week was a very difficult time for us, and we were certain that Jack's biopsy results would indicate that he had a neuroblastoma or ewing sarcoma. The pediatric oncologists were certain due to the location and mapping of the tumor that it was most likely going to be one of these types of cancer. We had already geared our minds to hope for the best, but we were beginning to resign ourselves to the fact that Jack would die before us. And, it was a tough pill to swallow.

When Jack's primary oncologist entered the room to give us the results of the biopsy, we were a bundle of nerves. When the conversation started out with "I have some good news," we couldn't believe our ears. Although these types of cancers almost never manifest themselves in the form of a growth, the biopsy results indicated the cancer cells were immature B-cell lymphocytes. The doctor continued to tell us these cells were more consistent with a lymphoma or a leukemia cancer diagnosis. The doctor stated these types of cancers have a 96-97 percent survival rate for children in Jack's age range. The doctor stated she thought the final result would be lymphoma due to the tumor. Later, we were even more surprised to find out that he had B-ALL (Acute Lymphoblastic Leukemia), which is the most curable form of childhood cancer.

But, how could this be? Oncologists are experts on these types of things. How could they have been wrong? Everything about the preliminary findings in Jack's case pointed to a much more severe type of cancer. The cancer was wrapped around the spinal cord which indicated neurological involvement (consistent with a neuroblastoma). In addition, it was a tumor. If you read up on leukemia, leukemia does not typically form tumors. It is a cancer of the blood, so the cancer is focused in the periphery blood and bone marrow which does not result in tumors. Even more baffling, Jack's leukemia diagnosis should have meant there was leukemia cancer cells in his blood. However, when they tested Jack's blood to identify these cancer cells, there were not any cancer cells present in his blood. All the cancer cells were concentrated in one area of his body.

I was sure of the answer to these questions. However, I was afraid to say it out loud at the time for fear of sounding insane. Maybe the cancer was originally a neuroblastoma. Maybe the united positivity and prayers of numerous people across the country resulted in a miracle. I was unsure how it could happen, but I strongly felt that this was the truth. Somehow, the powerful light in all these people created a powerful surge of positive energy focused on Jack, and transformed the cancer cells into a much more positive diagnosis. I now had a renewed hope. Although cancer treatment is no picnic, there was a good chance that I would not survive my son. And, it was the answer to all my prayers.

It is my belief that there is a powerful light within all of us (which is part of our Source). This powerful energy can be utilized at any time, although most of us have forgotten how to use it. However, sometimes when something extremely painful happens, we instinctively know where to find the power to heal it (even if we do not realize the mechanism for healing quite yet). Since this same light lies within everyone, it becomes even more powerful when we join together in a mutual desire. When people remember this light within themselves and focus this positive energy, the result is always a miracle. In the world of form, this miracle can appear in several different ways. In our situation, it gave Jack a fighting chance. It transmuted the cancer cells into something more survivable. It gave us something that we had lost and thought we would never find again. It gave us hope.

CHAPTER 4

The Next Chapter

The most difficult part of Jack's cancer treatment lasted approximately nine months and culminated into a rough end to the year 2015 and beginning of 2016. Jack was so nauseous that he sometimes had problems swallowing his medications. When he began chemotherapy on his birthday in May 2015, he weighed 70 pounds. By just after Christmas of 2015, he was down to 45 pounds. His skin was very pale and he had dark circles under his eyes. His body was a ghost of his former self. Throughout this time, I spent most of my time rubbing his sore legs and praying over him. I would sit at the end of his bed for hours, praying and rubbing his feet. It seemed to comfort him through the pain and discomfort he was going through.

When he felt well enough, I would read to him. When he felt particularly well, he would ride his scooter outside, or I would take him to the park to try to help him rebuild his strength. On October 28, 2015, we had a day where he was feeling well enough to ride his scooter. Despite the gloomy weather outside, he was determined to get some fresh air. For the entirety of the scooter ride, the clouds were gray and there was a cool and constant English mist falling from the dark sky. I wrote about this walk in a Facebook post on the same date.

> Jack wanted to ride his scooter this morning. It was misting and windy, but he didn't mind. He kept making comments, "What a beautiful day for a walk," "The wind and mist feel nice on my

face," and "It's nice to have such a peaceful, quiet walk." He slowly and casually rode his scooter for 1.5 hours (as I walked beside him) saying, "I'm not ready to go home yet. I'm enjoying this nice day." Most of the rest of the walk was silent as though there were no words strong enough to express how he felt. He just continued onward with a sweet and knowing smile on his face, as though he discovered some secret that no one else could comprehend. And I'm reminded of how much he has grown since this has all begun in May. In the wake of all this turmoil, he has learned to appreciate the little things. A peaceful walk, the rain and a strong wind in his face, and feeling well enough to ride his scooter for this long today (and taking in every moment of it.) All of these things...a reminder that he is alive...I doubt he will ever complain of a rainy day again. It brought me happiness to see the peace and enjoyment he was finding in the long scooter ride, and I wondered if most people ever appreciate such a simple moment in their own lives so completely and fully. I walked beside Jack with the same smile on my face...happy that he was so happy. And I realized he was teaching me what is truly important and meaningful during our walk. Perception is everything. You can choose to be happy no matter what circumstance may surround you. You can always see the silver lining. You can always embrace hope. -Facebook post October 2015

Despite all the terrible things Jack was experiencing at the time, this repetitious walk on the same path over and over again in our neighborhood will stand out in my mind for the rest of my life. He was so tired of lying in bed. He was so tired of not feeling well. He wanted a change of scenery so badly, that he decided to ride his scooter. The more he rode his scooter, the more energy he seemed to have. He didn't want to go home. He was fueled by the rainy mist and cool breezes. He had been in bed and indoors for so long that he forgot what it felt like to be alive. I think this scooter ride/walk reminded him how it felt to be alive again. It gave him a semblance of normalcy.

Jack could have chosen to stay in the house because of the poor weather conditions. He could have chosen to be sad. He could have chosen to be bitter at the world for his circumstances. But he chose to do the opposite. He chose to embrace the day and enjoy it to the fullest, despite the circumstances that surrounded him. He chose to rise up and meet the day with every fiber of his being. Where most people would have complained about the cool breeze and the non-stop mist falling from the sky, Jack witnessed the beauty in everything around him. The beauty of the day seemed to move through him and around him. His utter peace was so marked, that it was contagious. The peace he was feeling saturated my being as well. It was the most beautiful moment I have ever spent with another human being. To be in the presence of such positivity during such a dark chapter in his life was so truly amazing that it is hard to place into words.

That day, Jack's experience taught me to attempt to rise above the sadness and depression in our situation. Formerly, when I looked at Jack during that time, it made me sad to see the gauntness in his face and his sallow expressions. I used to think he looked like skin stretched over a skeleton, and it filled me with such despair. I would cry often. The sadness would overcome me, and I would run upstairs to my bedroom and sob. It broke my heart and my spirit to see my son in this condition.

However, after our walk that day, I chose to look at Jack with a new set of lenses. Instead of seeing a child having a near death experience, I saw a child that was powerful and filled with light. When I looked at his body, I chose to look deeper into his soul instead. That place was so strong, so peaceful, so calm, and full of so much healing. This was the new way I chose to look at my son throughout the rest of his cancer treatment. The truth and the light within every person and every object on Earth are all around us if we choose to see it. It just depends on what pair of lenses we choose to look through on any given day. We see what we want to see.

On a cold, misty morning, Jack's eyes witnessed a peaceful, unexplainable calm that filled his inner being and gave him strength. If he could summon the power to make this conscious visual transition, then I could too. I could choose to see the rainbow instead of the storm clouds behind it. After all, that same light is within all of us. I just needed to learn how to continuously acknowledge it. To keep that peace of mind at all times. I knew it would not be easy, but now I knew that it could be accomplished. My nine-year-old showed me that it was possible. He strengthened himself that day, but he also strengthened me on my life journey. He revealed a secret that I had forgotten. And I was so enamored of his courage and the peace that he projected, that I knew I wanted to feel that peace forever. It was a peace I wanted to learn to maintain and never forget again.

CHAPTER 5

A Rebirth

These two pictures show the difference between Jack during his most difficult time of therapy and Jack (now) on maintenance chemotherapy. Looking at him in January, I wondered if he would make it through or ever be the same. Although maintenance chemotherapy is far from normal, the transformation I have seen over the past two months has been amazing. He had gained 17 pounds since January, his hair is growing back, and he becomes stronger every day. It is no surprise to me that his hair is growing back in the same color it was at his birth (instead of the ash blonde it was at the time he was diagnosed, it is a light, reddish brown)...like a rebirth, a Phoenix being born again form the ashes. Marked by the pain and suffering he had to go through, but born anew. A higher power giving us a sign that the future ahead will be filled with more peaceful and happy times. I know we still have a long road ahead until his treatment ends in August 2018, but I wanted to share this transformation with all of you. For any of you who may be troubled or feeling lost, a sign of hope that you can be transformed as well. Love you all. -Facebook post on Easter Sunday 2016

*W*hen trauma strikes, it can be difficult to see the silver lining. However, difficult times do have the ability to bring about great transformation. It can become a shedding of the old self to make way for the new layers beneath. It is difficult for me to describe the pain and suffering I watched Jack undergo during his cancer treatment. Not only the physical pain, nausea, and discomfort, but also the suffering that ensued from not having the freedom to be a child. Cancer treatment brings so many restrictions. With the low immune system, he could no longer go to a movie theater or a crowded mall during flu season (which in Illinois is October – May). Nose bleeds came frequently and without warning. And when his fingernails and toenails began to fall off because of the strong chemotherapy, we placed Star Wars themed band-aids over them to help hold them in place.

Sometimes he would worry about being bald. Jack's father has shaved his head bald for years. He told Jack, "Hey, you will look just like me." This gave Jack comfort because belonging means to assimilate with your culture in even the smallest of ways, especially when you feel so different from everyone else. He would look like his Dad. He belonged in our small family subculture. It gave Jack peace. Sometimes he would worry about becoming too fat because of the puffiness the steroids caused. Any time he would have a pain in his knee, we would all fret that the cancer had returned to finish the job. To rob us of our son. To not only rob Jack of his childhood, but also his life. The gamut of emotions we all experienced were beyond painful. There's a heaviness in my heart as I recollect these memories even now. Sometimes I wonder how we all survived it. Sometimes I wonder if we will ever be the same again.

The answer is no. We will never be the same again. We will always be marked by this experience; however, we have the choice to change for the better. When Jack was admitted to the hospital for low white blood cell counts, we would always hope his counts would rebound quickly so we could return home. We all had our negative days. But it seemed like there was always one of us that could rise above it and assist in raising the spirits of the group.

Negative talk: "My counts will never go back up."

Positive response: "Yes, they will. I have a good feeling about it."

Negative talk: "This chemotherapy made him so sick last time. It will probably do the same thing again."

Positive response: "No, not this time. We are learning the nuances of his body better now. I think we can make better use of some of the anti-nausea medicines to move him through it with more comfort."

Maybe we didn't all recognize it at the time, but minute by minute, we were choosing how this experience would mold us into something new. Our old selves were gone. We would never be the same again. When you reach a point in your life where you feel the lowest you have ever felt, there has to be a moment when you decide to reach up and hope there is a hand to assist you. Sometimes choosing an optimistic mindset was a minute to minute battle; and, at other times, we were able to maintain a positive mental state for a couple days. We learned to extend space to one another when it was necessary, and we learned to speak positive, uplifting, loving words to one another when they were needed the most.

The alternative was not an option. Choosing negative talk and a gloomy, depressive state of mind would have only made an already terrible situation worse. And, when the three of us were stuck in a small hospital room together, cracking jokes, listening to music, and acting outright goofy were the only things that gave us any semblance of sanity. Anything that would remind us how to be happy, joyous, and wholehearted.

And that's how positive transformation happens, just a little bit at a time. Sometimes it takes a hefty dose of reprogramming our negative thought patterns, but we are all capable of making this transition. Sometimes we just need to access the bravery and courage that resides in every one of us in order to push-start the positive change. Once you choose to act on it consistently, it becomes a habit (just like riding a bike) and the day takes on a light and breezy feel. It was battling through negative self-talk that assisted us in making our transformation a positive one.

It was particularly joyous for me to post the above post on Facebook. There is an internal transformation that takes place when we choose the path to light. Jack's internal transformation was so bright that it burst through the 40-pound, skinny, pale façade, and uncovered a healthy, strong boy underneath. Within three months after the worst part of his treatment, his body was rebounding in wonderful ways. And, as his body became stronger, we all became stronger as witnesses to his improved health. And as the positive talk continued, our minds and spirits continued to grow stronger to guide us through the rest of his cancer treatment.

CHAPTER 6

Milestones — No Matter how Small

Yesterday, marked our two-year countdown to the end of Jack's cancer treatment. Last year, at this time, we began the high dose methotrexate treatments where Jack had to be hospitalized. This year, Jack is able to play outside, swim, and go to school. Life doesn't always give us promises of happy endings and perfection, but it does give the opportunity for us to create space for ourselves and reflect on the more important things in life. During this time of reflection, I am feeling thoughtful, thankful, and peaceful that whatever the future brings, we will forever look on the world with a new set of eyes. No matter what your situation brings you today, keep smiling, be centered, fill yourself with hope. As always, love to you all for your continued love and support. And, let the two-year countdown, which will bring an end to Jack's cancer treatment on August 27, 2018, begin! -Facebook post August 28, 2016

*W*hen faced with the nastiness of cancer treatment, we quickly learned we needed to take things a day (or sometimes a minute) at a time. It was easy to become overwhelmed by all the medications, hospital stays, and sleepless nights. It was easy to become saddened by the appearance of my pale, anemic son (especially when he was not able to enjoy the small things other children could enjoy every day). It was easy to quickly plummet into that slippery slope of "poor me" or "poor Jack."

When Jack was having a good day, we rejoiced. When he was having a bad day, we digested time minute by minute. We were doing the best we could to form a positive outlook. I made it my goal to attempt to be lighthearted despite the negative situation. Some days I was more successful than others. I was thankful to have my husband to help us through these moments. On the days I was barely making it, my husband seemed to catch the "positivity bug," and carry us through the negativity. Then, there were days when the roles were reversed. And, sometimes, when my husband and I were both down, Jack would say something hilarious (and we would all bust out laughing). Positivity is contagious. When one person can pull themselves out of the dark, the light they expose can fill an entire room with joy. It is impossible to be present in a room full of light and not feel the happiness surrounding you.

When I was struggling with keeping a positive focus or I could feel my mood darken, sometimes it was necessary for me to remove myself from the situation. I was very thankful for the meditation room on the fourth floor of the hospital. It gave me a place of reprieve during our hospital stays in moments when I was unable to move past dark thoughts. I was thankful for a porch swing my mother purchased for me for my birthday. When my mood would darken at home, I could walk outside onto the front porch and have a quiet place to sit. It was extremely therapeutic for me to quiet my mind. When my spirits were down, it was usually because of the endless "what if" thoughts that were buzzing through my mind.

"What if Jack has one of the severe side effects to this type of chemotherapy?"

"Oh my God. Someone just coughed on me in the hallway. I

will be so angry if I become sick and pass this on to my son with his lowered immune system."

"That's a new doctor. What if he/she doesn't know Jack's body well? What if he/she didn't read the chart. What if he/she makes a mistake?"

The only way I could calm this "mind chatter" was through a practice of quieting the mind through meditation. Sometimes, I would enter the meditation room, and the "mind chatter" would keep rambling on.

"Don't these thoughts know I have no interest in what they have to say? Why won't these dark thoughts just go away? I don't want them. Shoo, beat it," I thought.

On the particularly bad days (when I had troubles focusing), I would choose a word that would remind me of my "happy place" and repeat it slowly in my mind over and over again. Peace, Love, Kindness, any word at all. I found this practice helped me with the initial quieting of the mind. And when I was successful in stilling the mind completely (even for only a few minutes), the effects were phenomenal. A few minutes of mind stillness would "reset" the programming in my brain and give me the space and allowance to enter a more joyful frame of mind.

"Be gone, negative thoughts! You do not serve me anymore!" I would proclaim after a good meditation session.

Then, I could return to the hospital room (or indoors at home) with a better state of mind. On the days that we were able to maintain a positive mindset, it really made a difference in how well we were able to handle the situation (no matter how difficult it appeared to be on the outside). On the days that I was not able to maintain a positive mindset for very long, I learned to be patient with myself. Being frustrated and upset in that moment did not have to translate into experiencing the same frustration and upset the next hour, the next day, or the next week. Sometimes, I would gaze at Jack and attempt to see the light within him. To witness that part of him which would always remain invincible no matter what happened to his body. This imagery would help me interrupt some of the negative thought patterns.

In the above post, Jack still had two years of maintenance chemotherapy cancer treatment left. I could have written a post about the overall tremendous length of Jack's cancer treatment (3 ¼ years), and how distant the end of treatment appeared to be. However, it was more beneficial for me to speak loudly of what we accomplished, of how far we had come, of the grateful tenderness that ensued despite all the painful experiences.

"I am happy Jack is receiving maintenance chemotherapy right now instead of the hard chemotherapy he had to endure the first eight months."

"I am grateful Jack has felt well enough to play outside with friends today."

"I am fortunate that Jack's cancer is gone. This treatment is just to ensure it does not return."

Take it a step at a time, find something positive to say, learn to focus and quiet your mind from needless chatter. These were mindsets I learned to develop in order to survive the toughest times and make it through another day. Another example below:

Jack update: Yesterday, we turned a corner. We have the vomiting managed now, and he was able to eat a little bit and keep fluids down. He was even feeling well enough to sit up and play on his computer and hang out with his buddy, Sam. Lots of meds to keep the nausea under control, but it's working. He has chemo at St. Jude's tomorrow. Send positive thoughts his way. Chances are the chemo will hit him a little harder than usual since he's fighting a bacterial infection as well. He told me that he is going to his 5th grade graduation on Thursday no matter how bad he feels. Hoping for the best,

happy for the improvement. I will keep you all
updated. -Facebook post May 17, 2017

Cancer treatment is no picnic, and there are many feelings of sadness, helplessness, and hopeless that can sometimes surround it. When things were going badly, Jack always seemed to have something funny to say or he would make a statement with steadfast determination. In the above post, it was, "I am going to my 5th grade graduation no matter what!" Children are so resilient. And when Jack had enough of cancer controlling his life, he would make a positive affirmation like the one above and say it repeatedly. He was literally willing the positive thoughts into reality. And, yes, he did make it to his 5th grade graduation.

Jack made other funny statements to aid us in overcoming poor mood and bad attitude along the way. Jack was particularly nervous about his first surgery and being "put to sleep" by the doctors. Before his first surgery, he sang, *Highway to Hell* by AC/DC as he was being wheeled down the hall in his wheelchair for surgery. Laughter ensued.

Before one of Jack's many intrathecal methotrexate procedures (chemotherapy introduced into the spinal fluid), he told an entire room of doctors and nurses, "Just so you all know... you are in the presence of a verified YouTuber." Laughter ensued.

One day at the doctor's office, Jack's primary oncologist asked him if he had any questions. "Yep," he said. "Have you ever had a tumor?" The doctor explained that she had never had a tumor. "Well, how do you know so much about them then," was Jack's reply. The doctor laughed and said she studied about them in medical school with her pet dog. "Hmm," Jack said. "Well, what about your dog? Did he have a tumor then?" The doctor laughed again and explained that her dog never had a tumor either. Laughter ensued.

We had a "puke bowl" located in the living room by the couch where Jack spent most of his time during the tough part of chemotherapy treatment. One day, he was wearing the clean "puke bowl" on his head as a hat.

I asked him, "Jack, do you think it is a good idea to wear your puke bowl on your head?"

"Yeah, it's stylish," Jack replied.

I asked, "Where are you going to throw up if you get nauseous?"

"On you," he replied with a devious smile. Laughter ensued.

There were many times when Jack would take a fearful situation and find a way to make it more bearable. And, although, we aren't as funny as Jack, sometimes my husband and I would find something funny to say to ease the tension as well. We cannot always choose our circumstances, but we always can choose our attitude about them.

As we were moving through this difficult part of our life journey, we learned many lessons as well:

> Today marks one year to the end of Jack's cancer treatment. It is hard to believe that Jack has been fighting leukemia for well over two years now. It hasn't been easy, but I/we have learned many lessons along the way.
>
> To accept what I have no control over and cannot change and to learn to find peace and positivity in every moment. I may have no control over my situation, but I have control over how I react to it. I have learned to change my perspective and look at the world with a new set of lenses. To find peace where I formerly saw pain.
>
> When times are tough, to not look into the future and dwell on how far we have to go and wish it were all over. But, instead, choose to focus on the present moment. And move through the

difficult times a day, an hour, or a minute at a time.

To learn to trust ourselves and others. To have faith in the people surrounding us as well as in ourselves. To recognize the love and support we have from the surrounding community and learning to accept help when we need it.

To take meaning away from the things that ultimately have no meaning. Sometimes I have been guilty of placing importance in areas of my life that really don't matter all that much. To choose to let go of this concept and to find happiness in the given moment instead of looking for it in the past or the future.

To make space for myself. To know when I'm having difficulty staying positive and holding on to negative thoughts instead. To recognize these moments when my negativity is just making things worse and making the choice to separate myself...to take a walk around the block or sit in my porch swing listening to music. To gain a fresh perspective so I can go back to the stressful situation with a fresh outlook.

Throughout the next year, it will be my goal to focus on Jack's needs day to day. And, to not focus on possible negative outcomes (i.e. will it be a bad flu season, will there be a relapse, etc.). I look forward to the time that Jack's treatment is over, but I don't want to focus so much on the future that I forget to give him the love, support, and kindness he needs now to get through his cancer treatment day to day.

Taking it a day at a time...Let the countdown begin!! -Facebook post August 27, 2017

CHAPTER 7

Learning to be Gentle with Yourself

Sometimes staying positive is easier said than done. Especially, when emotions are running high and your life becomes that whirlwind of chaos that leaves you directionless. I often struggled with this on our journey with Jack's cancer treatment. An example in the below Facebook post:

> Jack has had pain in his right arm for about three weeks now. The pain was bad enough this morning that it woke him up.
>
> So, trip to St. Jude's today. Lots of tests. Ruled out a fracture (I guess the steroids weaken the bones, so they fracture easily.)
>
> Checked for blood clots through a couple of ultrasound tests. No result yet.
>
> His doctor seemed to think it is probably a joint impingement and she doesn't seem worried. (Apparently, five hours of Super Mario Galaxy on the WII could cause a repetitive movement injury).
>
> So, all around, nothing big right now.
>
> But I would be lying to you if I told you this wasn't scary. It closely mirrored the original symptoms of what led to his cancer diagnosis. I immediately feared a relapse.

Funny, how three years ago, I would have given him Tylenol and told him to rest it. Now, my mind quickly goes to a dark place.

A good reminder for me today to remain neutral in my analysis of a situation until I have all the information I need to interpret it.

To not upset myself with what could happen, but to remain focused on the present situation instead. Taking it in a moment at a time instead of trying to digest negative future possibilities in one gulp. Only to realize later I experienced all that fear and worry needlessly.

If the worst would have happened, then I would have had to accept it, but maybe I would have been better equipped to deal with the situation by not filling my mind with those negative thoughts.

I'm still learning, people. -Facebook post October 4, 2017

It is easy to tell myself that I should attempt to maintain positive thoughts despite what is going on around me; however, I am human. In this human experience, I am imperfect. And although I try to maintain a positive attitude, this is not always possible. Sometimes I fail in my efforts. I believe we are placed on this planet to learn life lessons. These life lessons include learning to forgive and love others, but also learning to forgive and love ourselves.

So, what do we do when we fail to maintain positive thoughts and self-talk? We learn to be gentle with ourselves. We learn to forgive ourselves and try again. If we make positive thoughts a habit, then the more we attempt to accomplish this task, the more it will become an automatic response in our life situation. If we choose to "beat ourselves up" over the choice to be negative, then that only takes us down the slippery slope of self-loathing even deeper. Just say, "Stop. I chose to give meaning to a negative thought a minute ago, but NOW I am choosing to manifest a positive thought instead." Then, rejoice in the fact that you changed the negative behavior and turned it into a present moment of peaceful awareness.

At the beginning of Jack's treatment, I was filled with fear, anxiety, and all the "what ifs." There were many times when the sadness would overcome me. I would bury my emotions so that I would not have to feel the pain associated with them. When the body is experiencing something traumatic, it can only maintain a "normal" equilibrium for so long. My husband used to "see it coming." He would tell me, "Honey, you just need to separate yourself from the situation and go cry." He could sense it in the air like electricity when I reached the inability to hold back the dam of emotions any longer.

I would always tell him I didn't need to cry. That I was "strong" and "could handle anything." About an hour later, I was always in my bathroom crying my heart out. Not just gentle tears running down my face, but guttural sobs complete with snot bubbles protruding from my nose. I would cry so hard, the capillary blood vessels around my eyes would burst (and I would emerge from my bathroom with small bruises around my eyes). When I finally released all the pent-up emotion with my tears, my husband would say, "Kate, that is your reset. You always let it build up and that is the way your body releases it. After you cry, you always feel better."

This was hard for me to hear. In the past, I had always associated crying with weakness, but I was wrong. My husband was right. It was a needed release. But, through this, I also discovered that it wasn't healthy for me to bottle up emotions for great lengths of time before I finally released them. Maybe, I could learn to pay better attention to my feelings surrounding a situation and learn to forgive them as they were happening (instead of stuffing them in the "sock drawer" of my soul until the overflowing drawer burst open). I have practiced going within and tuning into my feelings about each daily situation that pops up from minute to minute and hour to hour. And I have found that the sooner I can forgive a situation, the better I feel.

In fact, recently, I asked my husband and son to help hold me accountable. I told them, "If I say something negative about myself, someone else, or any given situation, I want you to call me out on it." And do they ever. When I say, "I can't believe my butt is too big for this pair of pants," then my husband always follows up with, "I'm gonna call you out on that." Then, I laugh, because I asked him to remind me to practice positive talk. And respond, "Okay, okay. Well, these pants do not fit anymore, but I hate dieting. So, good news, I get to go buy a new pair of pants," or "I love my body no matter what. It is strong and healthy and beautiful, and I am thankful for it." The comments vary depending on my mood at the time. But the accountability helps remind me to switch my negative thinking patterns off and replace them with positive thinking patterns instead.

CHAPTER 8

The Small Things

On Wednesday, as were riding in the car to school, Jack tells me, "I can't believe it, Mom. I made it through the month of October without having to go to the hospital." Historically, since Jack has been diagnosed, October has been a rough month for us. October 2015: High dose methotrexate in the hospital for two weeks. October 2016: Bacteria in his Mediport which almost killed him.

Not only does it make me happy for Jack to have made it through October 2017 unscathed. But, it also makes me happy that he has developed an appreciation for the "small things." To me, this means his mind is healing along with his body.

To appreciate the "small things" is something some people never develop in an entire lifetime, and young Jack, has learned it at the age of 11.

The "small things" in life bring healing to every one of us. A hand on the shoulder when you are feeling alone, a kind word when you are having a bad day, an encouraging smile from a stranger, a joke when you really need to stop taking yourself so seriously and laugh.

These things are the essence of life.

Despite some of the terrible things Jack has had to experience, his awareness of the "small things" brings me hope. That these terrible things have transmuted into some amazing traits for him as a young boy. Thoughtfulness, compassion, and kindness. These things can heal in an instant. And my hope is that he will spread this awareness to others in his interactions with them. To heal them as well. Because, let's face it. We could all use a little healing in our lives.
--Facebook post November 5, 2017

Maybe life is not going the way we think it should. Maybe it is hard to trust that you are exactly where you need to be in your life journey at any given moment in time. Right where you are, as you are, so that you can learn the life lessons you need on your road to enlightenment. Jack's leukemia treatment lasted 3 ¼ years which is a long time to be in the gutter. I often wondered how we were going to accomplish this feat. It seemed like such a long time to endure the roller coaster of emotions and treatment woes that come along with cancer treatment.

One of the things that helped us as a family was learning to appreciate the small things. Learning to show gratitude for a "good day" when Jack was feeling better than usual. To celebrate if we had an extended period of time where Jack didn't have to be admitted into the hospital. To be grateful that the cancer treatment was working as it should and keeping Jack's body safe from a cancer relapse.

Some days, a "small thing" was walking outside or Jack feeling well enough to go to the neighborhood playground. Some days, a "small thing" was living amidst one of the worst flu seasons in 2017-18 and being grateful for the good fortune that Jack never became contaminated with the flu that season.

A "small thing" was a chance encounter I had with another

mother at the hospital. We met in the laundry room and had both been in the hospital for an extended stay with our sons. Her son was fighting leukemia too. We shared our son's cancer diagnosis stories and our faith in something larger than us protecting us and guiding us along the way. The conversation ended in tears and an endearing, fierce hug. Although we both intended to clean clothes that day, I don't believe laundry was a priority after our conversation. When we left that laundry room and went our separate ways, we felt connected to one another with the sameness of our life journeys. Two mothers with sons fighting the same battle. The sameness in our current life situations made us both feel less alone.

A "small thing" was stepping outside my back door just before Christmas Day when Jack was enduring the roughest part of his cancer treatment to see a lighted Christmas tree and presents for our family. My sister had decorated a Christmas tree and left presents underneath the tree for our family. A tea wreath for me, a Starbucks card and clothing for my husband, and a go-kart for Jack. Jack weighed only 45 pounds and did not have much energy at the time, but his face lit up when he saw the thoughtful presentation in the back yard. Not only did this gift enliven Jack but gave my husband and I something to be thankful and grateful for as well.

A "small thing" was receiving a gift basket of Mary Kay skincare products for dry skin when Jack's skin was becoming dry and cracked from the chemotherapy drugs. I felt as though our guardian angels were guiding others in the community regarding Jack's needs, and these people were following this divine guidance and giving Jack exactly what he needed throughout his cancer treatment.

A "small thing" was having a friend organize a platelet drive in our area for people to donate platelets to Jack when there was a shortage and he was in dire need of them. The number of people who donated to him was amazing and it literally saved his life. At the time, Jack needed at least one bag of platelets a day (this lasted for three weeks), and the doctor told us Red Cross had a severe shortage. Jack's need was so great, he received a bag of platelets that was about to expire designated for the Neonatal Intensive Care Unit babies (because his need for platelets for survival was deemed greater). Family, friends, and members of the community rushed to his aid and donated platelets immediately to Jack. They donated so many, that Jack couldn't use them all, and the platelets benefited other children fighting cancer and life-threatening diseases in the children's hospital during the platelet shortage.

And when I look back at some of these "small things," I realize how extremely large and empowering they were. I should really change the wording to "grand things" or "powerful lessons in gratitude." Without the unity and help of others, Jack's cancer treatment would not have been nearly as successful. Sometimes, we had to look deep for the "small things" in our lives, but most of the time, friends, family, and community would rise together and fill our life with the "small things" so we could push through another day.

CHAPTER 9

Connection with Everything
— You are not Alone

I look at the tree outside my window and wish I understood its language.

It stands, firmly in the ground, immovable.

A sunny, warm day passes,

The leaves absorb the heat and light,

And the tree is at peace.

A storm comes, causing its branches to sway violently,

But the tree does not worry.

It takes what comes and accepts it wholeheartedly.

The tree does not scream or cry or yell at God for its misfortunes.

It does not project fear or anxiety on the objects that surround it.

It does not worry that lightning might strike it and burn it to the ground.

It rests in utter stillness as a beacon for mankind.

I want to learn the tree's language. I want to know what it is saying to me with the rustling of its leaves and the creaking of its branches.

I want it to shout at me and teach me its wisdom.

But that is not the tree's way.

It maintains its existence and teaches quietly as an example.

It knows I will learn its language when I'm ready to hear.

And, it stands, rooted to the earth, looking on me patiently.

Until I can let go of my old language and learn a new one of peace and knowing.

-Facebook post November 12, 2017

I wrote the above poem when I was in a solemn mood looking outside my window at the trees outside. My mind was in a state of turmoil, but when I looked at the trees in my backyard, they seemed to have it all figured out. It was as though they were whispering to me, "You need to learn to be still."

"But I don't want to be still," my mind protested.

"Okay, then. Whenever you are ready, we will be here," seemed to be the trees reply.

The tree's strength and wisdom in its stillness and lack of busyness made me think the tree had all the conundrums of life solved. I was wishing for the same thing. Sometimes, the mind is busy, and talks us into a frenzy. If we can figure out how to arrive to a place of stillness, then we would discover much more about ourselves. The strength that we carry within is covered by the incessant chatter of the mind, so we become distracted from our strength and light which lies at the core of our being. Our true light is a small spark ready to be ignited into a roaring fire. That strength and light is ready for us to witness and recognize at any time. It waits patiently (as the tree waits in my poem above) for us to remember our truth and light.

Sometimes our mind chatter wants to tell us how small and weak we are. How we don't matter. This couldn't be further from the truth. I believe that a higher power (God, Pachamama, Atman, Yahweh, the name does not matter, they are all the same) placed a bit of him or herself into his/her creations. Therefore, if a piece of God is within us, and we learn to quiet our minds (through meditation, a walk, whatever calms your mind), then we would have an opportunity to remember this Higher Power within us.

With the remembering comes a feeling of insurmountable love and unsurpassed peace. If we truly believed this power and light endowed every being and everything on this planet, then we would never feel alone.

We could be present in a forest with no people but feel as though we are surrounded by friends. We could be sitting in our living rooms surrounded by furniture and feel surrounded by peace and limitless. We could be confident that when our loved ones appear to "die", that they only leave the husk of a body they borrowed for a short time. But their true self (an extension of their Source and Creator) lives on into eternity. So, we do not have to be bereft at their seeming "death." As soon as we have learned our forgiveness lessons in the world of form, we will leave our bodies behind and reunite with them again. It is helpful to remember while we are still inhabiting our bodies and seem to be separated from deceased loved ones, if part of our Source is within everything then we are constantly connected to these loved ones. No matter what appears to take form in the physical world.

Another reminder of connectedness occurred at a state park in the below Facebook post.

> Pere Marquette State Park weekend. There's nothing more healing than communing with nature. The breeze blowing through the tree's leaves whisper encouragement. The earth beneath the hiking path holds us up and reassures us we are following the correct life path. And the deer notices us and pauses...reminding us to pause, be still, and listen to our inner voice for guidance. -Facebook post October 15, 2017

The most difficult task in overcoming the busyness of the mind is finding the best tool for learning to make the mind quiet.

These mechanisms for quieting the mind vary from person to person. It is important for you to investigate and find which way works best for you. Currently, my favorite way to quiet the mind is to sit in a quiet room, play some gentle spa music, soften my eyes, and focus on each note of the music playing. When I focus on the gentle cadence of the music, then my mind calms. Soon, I forget there is music playing, and my mind finds a modality of stillness altogether.

When I rewind the hands of time to the years of my youth, I realize I used running as a process of quieting the mind. I would place my headphones in my ears (connected to my non-skipping, portable CD player), listen to the beats of the music, and sync the beating of my feet on the pavement to the sounds blaring through my headphones. The stomping of my feet against the hard ground had a rhythm similar to a heartbeat. It was soothing, and, soon, I couldn't hear the music, but just the rhythmic heartbeat sounds my feet were imitating. My mind was empty of everything else, and I found peace during these moments outdoors.

In the above Facebook post, we were staying in a cabin at Pere Marquette State Park for the weekend. When I was a child, my family would go to this same state park to hike. The concept of hiking with nature surrounding me was a comfort. When I hiked in nature as a child (and still do as an adult), my worries and anxieties would dissolve into the dirt path beneath my feet. I felt lighter and happier, a truer version of myself. As I hiked, I was overcome with the peace of the oneness within myself and the nature and wildlife around me. I was one with the birds chirping, I could imitate their song. I was one with the trees, I could be still and grounded. I was one with the deer, I could run gracefully through the woods with delight. To this day, if I am feeling blue, a nature stroll will always place my mind back on track.

Whatever means of quieting the mind that works for you, find it! If our minds are full of busy nonsense, then we will never be able to hear our inner voice. Our true inner voice is not the busyness, but the quiet, constant awareness that supersedes all understanding in this world. It is our higher self, our guardian angels, our spirit animals (whatever concept gives you peace). This is the voice we strive to hear when the world has gone mad with chaos and uncertainty. It is the voice that guides us home.

During Jack's cancer treatment, my husband and I had to make life or death decisions involving his health routinely. These decisions were guided by the expertise of the doctors and nurses. However, listening to that Higher Power proved to be the most fulfilling and accurate guide on how to proceed with Jack's constantly evolving treatment plan. If my mind was full of chaos, I could not hear that inner guidance and truth.

When I needed to make decisions regarding Jack's health, I would practice quieting the mind. Then, I would ask that Higher Power or Source, "What should we do?" The answer would always come swiftly. I knew when it was the right answer because the answer would give me peace. Sometimes that answer defied some of the advice we were given by doctors. Although it was difficult to go against some of the doctor's advice, I learned to trust my inner voice. There were times when I did not trust that inner voice and the results were never good. As Jack's treatment progressed, I listened to that inner guidance more and more. I learned to trust my gut. That Higher Power was the best guide to moving me through this difficult phase with less struggle and less resistance. This was an important lesson for me. The world does not always know what is best for my situation, but my Source and Creator always has the answer.

CHAPTER 10

The Golden Pond

You can lead a horse to water, but you can't make him drink. This old homage, in the attempt to help others on their life journeys, has been around for generations. And, with it, comes the frustrations of the person leading the horse by his bridle to the drinking source. Only to find that once you arrive at the beautiful, pure drinking source, the parched horse refuses to drink in the water's miraculous sustenance. Have you ever been the horse? Have you ever been led by another to the water source that could quench your thirst forever, but refuse to drink? I have been there countless times (too many to count, in fact). So, for you, me, and everyone who has been the horse, this story is for you.

There once was a small village surrounded by a mountainous countryside. The beauty of the town spread far and wide, and at one time, the town was densely populated due to the town's charm and the gorgeous nature which surrounded it. That is, until the pond appeared, and changed the lives of the townspeople forever.

How does a pond appear do you ask? The townspeople had the same question. One night as the sun set, the townspeople went to their beds to sleep and dream. Most of them were sleeping soundly until a light flooded the interior of their homes. The light was so intense, people began pouring out of their homes to see what was happening. In the distance, the townspeople could see the source of the bright light. It was gold in color and shone like a beacon in the distance. It was as bright as the sun and made it difficult for anyone to return to their dream haven.

Although it was late at night, the townspeople held an emergency meeting in the town square in regards to the peculiar light. It was decided two brave men and two brave women would head towards the light source and investigate. So, away they went towards the beacon in the night not knowing what they would find. The rest of the townspeople stayed huddled in the town square to wait. When the four adventurous souls returned, they were changed. They were light and airy, giggling and full of joy. They told the rest of the townspeople that they located a "golden" pond about five miles outside of town. Everyone was confused. Many had traveled the area surrounding their town and never seen a pond. Some of the people immediately disbelieved them.

One man said, "Whatever they found must be dangerous. It has changed their personalities and caused them to hallucinate. There is no pond five miles outside of town. If that were the case, one of us would have seen it by now. The light source has driven them mad. We should all stay away from it."

But, then, each member of the brave quartet countered, "No, it was the most beautiful thing we have ever seen."

"Yes, yes," another brave adventurer said. "You all must go and see for yourself."

"Please do," another joined in. "When you look into the light of the pond....." His voice trailed off. "Well, I just can't describe it or put it into words. It is amazing. You all must go and see."

Another townsperson who stayed in the village while the party of four investigated spoke up next. "The light IS dangerous. It is trickery of some sort. It has cast a spell on those who have seen it. We must all stay away from it."

The townsperson next to him added, "Yes, yes, we should make a law forbidding anyone to walk towards the strange light."

The Mayor of the town agreed and decried no one should approach the glowing light under any circumstance. The four adventurers tried to protest, but their voices were drowned out by the rest of the townspeople.

For several weeks, no one spoke of the light. People began placing dark covers over their windows, so they were able to sleep at night. The four people who investigated the source of the light were considered mad and treated poorly by the rest of the townspeople.

But, as the days passed, there were some people that were curious about what the four seekers had discovered, and, in secret, ventured towards the peculiar light. When they returned to the village, they were changed people. They were light-hearted and full of joy. Despite the jeers and bad talk from other villagers, those who looked upon the pond were resistant to any negativity whatsoever.

Soon, the party of four and the curious people who followed in their footsteps discovered they had "outgrown" the town. Despite the heavenly landscapes which surrounded the town, they knew they needed to move on. Therefore, they left the town.

As the number of people leaving the town increased, the Mayor made a new decry. He commanded that a 100-foot brick wall be built around the golden pond in order to protect the remaining citizens from their own curiosities regarding the bewildering light. The Mayor made those building the wall wear a special form of glasses that eliminated most of the light and told the builders under no circumstances were they to look directly at the pond. Most of the builders listened to the Mayor's instructions; however, a few looked into the pond instead. Those who looked into the pond never returned to the village.

Once the wall was built, the remaining people in the village became accustomed to the nightly beacon and it was spoke of very little. Many of them thought if they never spoke of it, then maybe it never happened. With the massive wall to deter anyone from entering the area of the pond, those that were curious soon realized it would be impossible to scale the wall and gave up on the idea. The Mayor was pleased with his decision.

Fifty years passed, and no one spoke a word of the golden pond. In fact, most of the remaining townspeople became so accustomed to it, they didn't even notice it existed. They looked upon it as they would a tree in their front yard or a rabbit hopping across the grass. Just a part of the scenery, a constant in their lives so familiar it was concealed in plain view.

One day, a fifteen-year-old boy asked his father, "What is that light in the distance? I know it has always been here, but it calls to me. No one ever speaks of it. Has it always been here?"

The father replied, "What light are you talking about?"

The curious boy responded, "You know. The really bright one that keeps me awake all night."

"Well, it shouldn't keep you awake all night if you use your bedroom curtains properly," the father said.

"Yes, I know. But there was one night when I didn't close the curtains tightly enough. It looked like there was a gold outline around my bed curtains. It was beautiful and made me curious. So, I opened the curtains completely, and looked at the golden light in the distance. It really is marvelous, but no one ever speaks of it," the boy said.

"There is nothing marvelous about that light," the father replied. "It just appeared when I was a child. I remember my grandparents telling me to stay away from it. I think it is haunted or bewitched or something."

"Well, how do you know?" the boy questioned.

"I don't know. Just the stories I heard as a child. Something about the light appearing and people going to investigate the source. Something about a pond that caused them to hallucinate badly. It was said that anyone who looked at the pond would go mad. Most of the people who looked at the pond disappeared from the town entirely. The Mayor built a 100-foot brick wall around it to keep people away," the boy's father said.

"Well, Dad. Did you ever see the pond?" the boy asked.

"No," the father replied.

"Have you ever spoken to anyone who has seen the pond?" the boy questioned further.

"No," the father replied again.

"Then, how do you know the story is true?" the boy asked.

The boy's father was becoming agitated, "Because that is the story I was told. Anyway, if the pond wasn't dangerous, then why would someone build a wall around it? I don't want to hear any more questions about the golden pond. I could probably get in trouble for just talking about it. No one in this town even acknowledges its existence anymore. They just carry on as though it never appeared out of thin air, as though it doesn't attempt to light up our rooms at night, as though it doesn't even exist."

"Dad, have you ever wanted to go and look at the pond?" the boy asked.

"What did I say about questions about the pond?" the father replied with a stern look.

"Okay. No more questions then," the boy replied sullenly.

No matter how hard he tried, the boy could not remove the concept of a golden pond out of his mind. He couldn't believe that something so beautiful and pure looking could be evil. So, one night he left his house to do the unthinkable. To climb the wall surrounding the pond. The boy wasn't sure how he was going to accomplish the task, but he wanted to try. As he approached the strange golden illumination, he couldn't help but be intimidated by the seemingly impenetrable wall. The Mayor had certainly made it difficult for anyone to scale its enormity. The boy walked around the entire wall looking for possible weaknesses to its structure. He could find none. Just as the boy was about to give up, something appeared out of the corner of his eye. It was a golden ladder.

At first, the boy thought he must have gone mad, but as he approached the ladder, it was solid and tall enough to scale the wall. The boy could hear his father's voice in his head about the pond being evil and driving people out of their right minds. Although the boy was a little frightened by the magical ladder, he had gone too far to stop now.

He hoisted the ladder up against the wall and began to climb. When he reached the top of the ladder, he gazed at what lay behind the wall. It was a golden pond. It was translucent and deep. It emitted a strong light source from its surface. However, it was not like a normal pond. A normal pond would have reflected the stars in the night sky, the majestic willow trees that surrounded it, and the barriers of the wall on its surface.

This pond didn't appear to reflect anything. Its surface was clear of any type of image. Only the light shone from its glassy unspoiled surface.

When the boy looked at the pond, he was not filled with fear, but filled with wonderment. He hoisted the ladder to the other side of the wall, so he could climb down and come into contact with the pond's unquestionable beauty. As he approached the bank of the pond, he instinctually looked into the pond's surface. He expected to see a reflection of himself, but there was no reflection there. Only the brilliant bright light. The light reached up from the surface of the pond and touched the center of his forehead. When this happened, the boy immediately had an epiphany. The light didn't reflect any images because it was reflecting the truth. The boy was the light. The tree was the light. The wall was the light. Each star in the night sky was the light. All connected. All one with each other. They may have taken different forms in this world, but the pond reflected their true identities. This revelation brought tears to the boy's eyes. He had never felt so loved and connected with the world around him in his entire life. The truth the pond showed him changed him forever. He would forever be filled with gratitude and joy for the truth that surrounded him. For his remaining years on Earth, he would always look past each seemingly separate object on his path and see the light and connectivity within instead.

As we walk along our lifepaths, sometimes we do not realize how much societal norms and our upbringing as children affect our perception of the world in which we live. There are many "truths" we are taught as children that are quite the opposite of truth. For example, the societal "truth" that we would all be happier if we morphed our personalities into the personalities of others (so we can "fit in"). Of course, this is a lie. We are much happier when we allow ourselves to be how we were created. We are happier when we are able to express our creativity and gifts and allow our personalities to grow and move along its appointed path. In fact, we become depressed when we repress who we are. It is confusing for people to pretend to be someone they are not in order to keep society and the rest of the world happy. "Why can't I just be as I am. Isn't **who** I am, **as** I am, good enough?"

It is the same with the story about the golden pond. Society is preaching what is best for the people by building a wall; however, many of the people knew the truth within their hearts. They knew the pond was a miracle for them to explore. In addition, the pond's emergence was a sign that many people in this town were ready to grow and expand their spiritual horizons and knowledge of the Universe. Those people brave enough to move towards the light despite the cautions of the Mayor became enlightened. The pond was an explanation of their truth and these people were ready to listen. They were ready to allow themselves to be transformed. They were ready to step outside of the societal norm in order to embrace their truth and find true happiness. They were tired of the old story. They were tired of trying to "fit in" within a community where their gifts were often hidden and squandered. That is why the golden pond beckoned to those people.

There comes a time in our spiritual journey where we need to leave old ideas behind in order to grow. This can be so difficult because we have been taught our entire lives how important it is to assimilate into the culture in which we were brought up in. Society can teach us many truths depending on what community we were raised in. Sometimes, society teaches us to be kind. Sometimes, society teaches us to help others. Sometimes, society teaches us to love and accept people different than we are. These things give us permission to be ourselves and allow us to evolve into something more. But when some of the societal norms no longer fit with who we want to be, then it is time to leave the village and move on to greener pastures. If the former community taught you well, then you can bring the positive lessons with you. But if a community is stifling your growth, then you need to be brave enough to leave when you hear the call.

What about the societal norms that are not in alignment with our spiritual truth. For example, society tells us we should look "perfect," so we work out incessantly and schedule plastic surgery. We sacrifice our minds, hearts, and souls for our bodies. We look to the outside to meet our inner needs instead of looking within which is the only place these inner needs can be met.

Sometimes society tells us we should continuously sacrifice ourselves for the sake of others. However, if we don't work to meet our own needs, we have nothing to give to others. It is the cycle of giving and receiving. We can't give people what we don't have. When we are only giving, but not receiving, it's like handing someone an empty cup. Your cup is empty because you have given everything away, but never bothered to refill it. But when we receive from others, our cup is filled. So we have something to give others when they need it (completing the cycle of giving and receiving).

Sometimes society tells us we should strive to obtain a profession where we make large amounts of money. But in our myopic focus for what we think we should achieve, we forget about our spiritual path and are unhappy regardless of the amount of money we make. The physical objects in the outside world cannot meet the inner need for peace and completeness. Any time we make decisions out of alignment with our spiritual truth, we lead ourselves to a path of unhappiness, restlessness, and fear.

All these negative societal norms distract us from necessary change in growing into the person we were meant to be. We become so distracted by attempting to please society, we forget about our own spiritual path which is needed for our own happiness. We think by pleasing society, we will be happy because we think we will belong and "fit in." But if we don't feel free to be ourselves, to dig deep, and to discover more, then we are left feeling empty inside. Plus, the negative societal demands will keep changing, and it is exhausting to pretend to be someone else and to keep up with trying to meet the demands of the negative social standards.

It is difficult to give up the societal norms that do not match up with our inner truth because we want to belong to the community. We want love and acceptance from the people around us and we worry that we will lose that love and acceptance if we ditch the community standards that no longer sync up with our belief system. It takes great courage and trust in Spirit to move away from the old community mindsets in search for something new. As you change and outgrow the negative societal norms, it is paramount that you follow whatever guidance Spirit gives you (even if it diverges severely from what the collective societal mindset would have you achieve).

For those who were fearful of the golden pond, I understand completely. The golden pond represented letting go of the old self and old ideas which were deeply embedded in our psyche since birth. In our lifetime, we build this identity of ourselves through our experiences and the stories we are taught by our tribe or community. The thought of outgrowing the community which taught us "everything we know" is frightening. We question, "Who will be our new teacher?" Building a trust with the unknown (the golden pond) begs the question, "Will the old self die if I pursue this? Can I survive without my community?"

The truth is that some of the people in your life will follow you on this journey because they are ready for the change in perspective too. However, some may need to be left behind. Not because you do not love them and appreciate them, but because a fork in the road has developed in your relationship. This fork has two directions. Your heart is begging you to go right and the other person's heart is not ready to go right yet. For the other person, left seems like a safer path. Then, you are faced with the decision, "Can I let go of this person in my life? Do I go left too so I do not lose this person in my life?" Although it is a difficult decision, going left would only remove you from your path and leave you unsatisfied and unhappy. When your heart is telling you to journey in a new direction, it is important to listen and follow that path. Even if it defies societal norms.

You do not have to leave this loved one out of your life forever, but to not pursue the truth would be a disservice to you both. It is not fair for you to live a lie, and it is not fair to the loved one if you are pretending to be someone you are not. You must move in this direction and trust there is a Higher Power looking over you to guide the way. It is in your best interest to do so. Your love for your old community may remain, but you may need to move to a new community to further your growth. And, maybe, just maybe.... others will follow you from the old village eventually. When they are ready. Maybe your courage in seeking the unknown will be the push they need to uncover their soul selves.

CHAPTER 11

Why Pain???

Why does pain have to be a part of our life journey? Although it takes many forms, the bodily response to pain is the same for all of us. It is that heaviness in our chest. It feels as though there is a 5-gallon pitcher of water resting on our lungs. We try desperately to stop breathing, for fear we may spill the water and allow it to flow over us. But what is it that we fear? Why are we afraid to let go of this pain? Taking a deep breath and allowing the 5-gallon pitcher to empty would lighten our load, yet we choose to remain uncomfortable and hold it there. We choose to take shallow breaths. Not allowing the added oxygen (our bodies badly need) to enter our lungs, to free us of this pain.

We are resistant to allow the pain to be a part of our life journey. Part of us would rather not release this pain. We would rather not soak ourselves with indignity as the pitcher of water empties and drenches our body. We convince ourselves that the volume of water in the pitcher is greater than it is, and we will never dry off if we allow it to spill. We think we will be endlessly uncomfortable with our saturated clothing sticking to our bodies when it empties. We convince ourselves the coolness of the water will give us hypothermia. We convince ourselves that we should balance the water on our chests precariously because someone else may need the water to drink. It would be wasteful and selfish to empty it. Despite the discomfort, we invent several different rationalizations to hold on to this pain.

The truth is that we have been accustomed to think that pain is part of our identity. We fear if we let go of this pain, we will let go of our very being. We will be nothing. We will cease to exist. And, so we live with the 5-gallon pitcher on our chest. Barely living, compromising our very existence because we fear a slight discomfort. We have learned to integrate our beings with this pain, to weave it into part of our identity. This limits our freedom. It restricts the light that exists in all of us. We must all learn to let go of this pain if we want to be free. However, this is not always easy.

We have accumulated this pain over an entire lifetime, and often over several lifetimes. The pain cycles have become a habit in our way of living, and it can be very difficult to break this habit. Sometimes, when I try to let go of pain, I feel as though I am asking myself to rip my still-beating heart out of my chest. I have made it a part of my identity. I have conditioned myself to run from the pain instead of confronting it. If I distract myself with other meaningless things, then maybe I will forget the heavy pitcher on my chest. But, ultimately, running from the pain only causes me to hold onto it, and not dispense of it appropriately. Then, as more painful events appear in my life, I have even more pain to release and remove from my psyche. Soon, what used to be the 5-gallon pitcher of water turns into Lake Michigan.

When pain accumulates to this point, it becomes impossible to carry ourselves through everyday life, let alone be able to take care of anyone else. We are so weighed down by the pain that it becomes difficult to move, to eat, or to take care of ourselves in any way whatsoever. This manifests feelings of depression, sadness, and helplessness. This is no way to live. Now, what would have been a mild discomfort of getting our clothes wet by letting go of the 5-gallon pitcher, we feel as though there is no escape. We feel as though we are drowning in a sea of pain. We don't remember how to swim, we don't have a boat, and we don't have a life vest. How much harder is it to let go of this pain now? It seems like an insurmountable task that cannot be accomplished. Therefore, it is important to let go of painful situations as quickly as possible. See it, acknowledge that it is part of your life journey, but recognize that it does not define you. Then, let it pass over you and through you. Clear your heart.

The month of May has been a rough month for Jack. With only three months left of treatment, we have hit another rough patch. We made it through one of the worst flu seasons in the past ten years, only to have Jack catch human pneumococcal virus which placed us in the hospital for a couple of days. The virus lowered his counts to the point where we couldn't be in public places for fear of a secondary infection.

We, gratefully, moved past this hurdle (confident this was our end-of-treatment-hiccup) only to run into another hurdle. After having several intrathecal chemotherapy procedures with no issues (well over 50 in the past three years), Jack has experienced some severe pain since his procedure on Wednesday. Jack jerked awake during his procedure with the needle in his spine. It was not safe to continue the procedure, so they had to remove the needle and stick another needle into his spine to complete the procedure.

Two hours after the procedure (about the time we arrived at home), Jack stood up to get out of the car and stated his hips hurt so bad, he wasn't sure he could walk. He told me he was afraid he was going to become paralyzed. The terrible pain started in his hips and radiated down the back of his legs. A day later, he had severe pain behind his eyes. After three days of phone calls with the doctor, and another visit to St. Jude's yesterday, we hope to have the problem diagnosed. It is likely when Jack's body jerked during the procedure that the needle agitated peripheral nerves surrounding the spinal cord (which is causing this pain). In addition, the doctors think Jack might have a spinal fluid leak which would cause the pain behind his eyes. They were able to make him comfortable with pain medications yesterday. The doctors said the nerve pain should go away on its own. The spinal fluid leak should repair itself on its own as well. If it does not get better by Tuesday, Jack will need to receive a blood patch to fix it. For a child that has had to endure so much pain during treatment, it is heartbreaking to see him go through more severe pain yet again.

During this week, I have come to the realization that I have not completely let go of the pain I have accumulated as a result of Jack's cancer treatment. I have been in the process of removing the 5-gallon pitcher of water from my chest a cup at a time (as I am able), but I have not fully released the entirety of the pitcher's contents. Poor Jack has had to endure the physical pain of a cancer patient. My husband and I have had to endure the emotional pain of watching our son move through this difficult part of his life journey.

After receiving the pain medication at clinic, Jack felt well enough to eat dinner at a restaurant last night. I think he could see the sadness on my face. I told him that I was so sorry he had to go through this pain. Jack said, "It's okay, Mom. Everyone experiences this pain at one time or another in life. I am just experiencing my pain a little earlier than most others. Maybe that will mean the rest of my life will be easier." As the pain was coursing through his body, Jack was choosing to let go of the pain with this statement. He was emptying his pitcher of water. He could have chosen to be bitter about having to go through cancer treatment at such a young age, but, in this moment, he chose to move through it and past it. He chose to let the pain go. As he was saying these words, I felt like he was giving me permission to let go of my emotional pain surrounding the last three years as well. I was grateful for it.

We need one another to ease the eradication of the pain cycle in our lives. Sometimes, maybe we need to witness the release of pain in another person. To see that they survived the process unscathed. This can give us the courage we need to remove pain from our hearts as well. In the past three years, there have been many times where I have felt like the parental roles have been reversed. There have been times when Jack has been the teacher and I have been the student. In moments like these, his positive perspective and insight has helped cure my negativity. I feel like my lesson in this circumstance is that conquering pain does not have to be a lonely task. Perhaps, togetherness and encouragement from others is an integral part of the process of pain removal from our lives. And, with guidance from one another, maybe we can steadily allow the pain of any given moment to move past us and through us instead of choosing to carry it within us. Together, maybe we can untie these bonds we have woven from our pain and be free. -Facebook post May 2018

*P*ain. It can manifest itself horribly in these physical bodies. But pain is not only limited to the physical body, but to our emotions, our mind, and our spirit as well. However, when I reflect on how pain has affected me in this lifetime, I can also say that it has given me an immense opportunity to transform in a positive way.

When Jack was diagnosed with cancer, I was devasted and in

the worst pain of my life. There were other times in my life where I may have had physical pain or emotional pain separately. But this pain was different, this pain saturated my body, heart, and soul. My entire being felt heavy like lead, as though it was a great burden to even move. Although this was in no way pleasant, this pervasive pain gave me only two options: I could choose to become bitter and hateful over what was happening to my son OR I could dig deep into my soul and start looking for the answers I needed to claw my way back up through the dirt.

I had seen other people in the hospital with a loved one suffering, and I noticed that some of them had chosen to be hateful and bitter. This is not a judgment. I was one of these people in the beginning too.

"Why me?"

"It isn't fair."

"Bad things only happen to me."

"It must be nice to be that person; their family member has a better chance of survival than mine."

Although it was tempting to fall into this trap, ultimately, none of these mindsets were in the least bit helpful to me. In fact, I decided that it would not only make things more difficult for me to poison my mind with helpless, hateful jargon, but it would also have a negative effect on Jack's treatment. If Jack heard me making these comments, then he might adopt the same attitude. And there's only one thing sadder than a child suffering, and that is a child suffering AND feeling sorry for him or herself. A child suffering and thinking the world owes him or her something because something bad has happened to them. The victim mentality can play out in all sorts of awful ways, and I didn't want my son to think that he was a victim. Along with that, I did not want to adopt a victim mentality myself. I did not want to feel sorry for myself. I knew it would not be easy, but I had to start searching for the truth.

For me, the truth came in a book called *Disappearance of*

the Universe by Gary Renard. My friend, Bev, lent me the book approximately one month after Jack was diagnosed. For me, as I read the pages of the book, I had known the contents of the pages had always been the truth. This book led me to study *A Course of Miracles* and the rest is history. For me, it was the most spiritually transformative experience to study the pages of these books. If you want to try these mediums, then go ahead. However, I am not urging you to take the same path that I took. This path was presented to me at a very hard time in my life, and I decided to give it a try. Whatever path is presented to you in your time of need, you should grab it by the hand and allow it to show you the way.

You may ask, "How do I know which path to take?" When it comes to uncovering and relying on a spiritual doctrine in your search, ask yourself, "Does this give me peace?" Then, attempt to assimilate that doctrine into your life experience. After you have done this, ask yourself, "Does this spiritual doctrine still give me peace?" If it does not, then it is time to keep searching. The doctrine and your life experience should assimilate peacefully. This does not mean that it will mesh with the overall world view or even be a popular thought amongst certain communities. Assimilating into someone else's world view is irrelevant. What is important is that the concepts contained in the doctrine fill YOU with peace. What is important is that the concepts assimilate well into YOUR world view and YOUR life. If your mindset can remain tranquil regardless of what may be happening around you, then you are on the right path. If you can love yourself without worry of judgment from others, then you are definitely on the right path.

Each person's path may take different roads, but these diverging paths are all guiding us to the same place. It is like walking in a maze with no dead ends. A different path is taken, but the outcome is always the same. We live in a world of duality where we have different personalities and different ways of learning and perceiving. The truth is (underneath all those differences) we are all the same. Just as our Source created us. However, in this world of duality, our differing personalities cause us to learn in different ways. Therefore, when you are struggling with a difficult time, it is tantamount that you quiet your mind and listen to your inner voice. Not the inner voice that gives you anxiety, fear, and panic. That is mind chatter. Mind chatter just distracts you from the truth.

When you can submerge into a state of mindlessness, you will hear your true voice. This voice is much more powerful than the mind chatter. You will recognize it immediately because it is a voice that will fill your being with peace and harmony. Listen to this voice, this is the voice that will be the guide on your path to your truth. And no way is the wrong way. Spirit will present itself to you in a way that you can best receive and accept. These ways are different for all of us, and there is no judgment for the way you choose to make this journey.

Just close your eyes, still your mind (in whatever way works for you best), and just ask for help. That's all you need to do. Just surrender your identity with past pain for the present moment, and I promise you that you will hear this voice. It may come as a voice or maybe just an idea in your head. But follow this direction when it presents itself because it is the voice guiding you to enlightenment. It is the voice leading you out of all pain. It is the voice that brings you back to your Spirit self.

For me, pain has brought about the most profound transformation. Because it is uncomfortable, it strongly urges me to find another way. Since I do not like the feelings pain provides, I look deeper for ways to release and find nourishment. Because I have hit rock bottom, I want to delve deep within myself for answers in order to lift me back up to my true identity, my true purpose, and my true home.

But sometimes there is inner resistance to releasing the pain. Like I mentioned in the Facebook post above, we make the pain a part of our identity. If we are in a state where we are finding it hard to let go of this pain, it is important not to judge ourselves. This judgment will only empower the painful situation. Instead, the only action we might be capable of doing in an immensely painful situation is surrounding the pain with acceptance. When we can fully accept the pain as it is in the present moment, then Spirit often will give us space enough around the pain in order to move through it more quickly. This might be a situation where we might not be able to experience peace and that is okay.

However, as we realize that every situation that we encounter in these physical bodies is a transitionary and temporary experience, then we know we will not be in this state of pain forever. If you cannot release the pain at the time, have patience with yourself. Ask Spirit for guidance. If you can release it a week later, then release it then. If you can release it a month later, then release it then. But make sure that you consciously choose to release it as you are ready. If you do not appropriately dispense of the pain, then you will continue to carry it in your body. And if you continue to carry it in your body, then you will experience the same pain again (probably in another form). Trust me. I have had to learn this the hard way.

You might ask, "How do I know that I have forgiven or released the pain?" For me, I can tell whether I have forgiven a painful situation or even a physical pain in the body when I can look back on the experience without grimacing. If I can look back on the situation, and not feel a semblance of the same pain, then I know I have released it. If I look back on a painful experience and see that I still have a strong emotional response to the pain, then I know that I still have work to do. The important thing is to be patient with yourself. Releasing pain that you have formed an identity around is not easy work, so always remember to be gentle with yourself.

As far as the pain that I have carried from Jack's cancer treatment, I can say that I have forgiven sections of the overall painful experience. However, when I remember some of the pain he has had to endure, I see that I still have work to do. Sometimes I will feel my body tense up at these thoughts, or I will feel anxiety and a heaviness in my chest. All I can do is be patient with myself. I know that if I judge myself, I am only causing resistance in releasing the pain. Again, this is not easy, but I am still continuing the work. Slowly, gently, until there is a time that the discomfort of these memories will be eliminated completely with a knowing that we all end up at the same place. I remember that no matter how much pain we experience on our journey, we all end up in the same realm of peace. And when I look at the miracles that Spirit has shown me this far, I know that if I am willing, I will receive the assistance I need to eliminate this pain completely from my life. And so, will you.

CHAPTER 12

Resistance to the Truth

This phrase keeps coming up in my everyday life lately. In a song, in a book I'm reading, on a television show. "The truth will set you free, but first it will piss you off."

When I hear this phrase, it reminds me of Plato's parable of *The Cave*. A group of people were imprisoned in a cave. They were bound so tightly to the wall that they couldn't even move their heads. All they could see were shadows on the wall of the cave. This became their new reality and they forgot who they once were. All they knew were the shadows that appeared before them on the wall. One day, one of the prisoners was able to escape and left the cave. He saw the real world around him and saw that the shadows on the wall of the cave were caused by people crossing through the light that shone into a crack in the cave wall. He was excited, yet fearful about this world and he ran back to the cave to free the other prisoners. When he told the other prisoners the truth about the shadows on the wall, they became angry. The free man attempted to free the other men, but they refused to accept the truth he provided them. They chose to stay chained to the wall instead and shouted hateful, cruel things to the free man until he was forced to leave.

The truth is that sometimes bad things happen, and sometimes we choose to let these things imprison us rather than using it as a mechanism for setting us free. Sometimes, even when we are given the opportunity to free ourselves, we are hesitant to do so. Maybe we think we aren't worthy of good things, maybe we are afraid of the unknown, maybe we have forgotten who we are. But, even though we cannot control what happens to us, we can still control how we react to it and how we will let it affect us.

I have gone through a metamorphosis in my perspective on life throughout Jack's cancer treatment. Particularly, in the way I react and process some of the bad things he has had to endure. Although it makes me sad that he has had to go through so much suffering at a young age, I have found that trying to stay positive and let go of this sadness has been more beneficial to our psyche as a family than choosing to hold on to these feelings of sadness and anxiety.

Although it makes me angry that any person should have to endure the suffering of a serious illness, I have made a choice to let go of that anger, anxiety, and fear. To free myself from that prison. I make this choice daily although it isn't easy. To hold onto this anger and sadness would only imprison myself and my ability to help Jack continue to heal. I am confident that this mindset will help us overcome difficult times, and will, essentially set us free. -Facebook post January 6, 2018

I read Plato's parable of *The Cave* while studying a philosophy class in college in the late 1990's, and I was reintroduced to the story while reading *Disappearance of the Universe* by Gary Renard. Sometimes on the journey to peace (because you have had enough of the suffering), you will find that people surrounding you are not ready to be on this journey. In fact, these people may be very proud of the prison walls they have built around themselves. It is important to allow these people space to be who they are in the present moment without judgment. Everyone comes around to the truth in their own way and in their own time. If they don't move towards their truth and oneness in this lifetime, then maybe they will decide to make the transition in the next lifetime. At some point, everyone becomes tired of the suffering.

A prison can be alluring especially if you do not view it as a prison. If you constructed the prison like a garden with a white picket fence around it, then maybe you have the perspective that your prison provides you with the beauty of flowers and the sustenance of fruits and vegetables. In fact, maybe your prison is exactly what you think you need. Perhaps, you have all the food your body could ever possibly need to stay healthy and strong. Maybe you constructed a fence so impenetrable that it will prevent all the pests from eating your crops. Maybe your garden gives you plenty of work to do, so you can distract yourself from worrying. Maybe you constructed your garden in a world where the sun always shines and there is never any inclement weather. Maybe you built a fortress blocking all people who might cause you harm. This doesn't seem so bad, does it?

You built the prison around you and you are quite fond of it. In fact, you can't even remember what is outside the prison, so the thought of deconstructing the prison is extremely fearful. If someone hung a sign on your garden fence door stating, "Poisoned vegetables. Scheduled for demolition," then this might bring you into a state of sheer panic. Everything you think that you know would be destroyed.

For this reason, people become very attached to the prisons they have constructed. These structures that they have built around them give them a false sense of safety. A scary idea is introduced to the person, and the person may think, "If my prison is destroyed, will I be destroyed along with it?" If a person is this identified with their prison, then you can see why the thought of setting the garden on fire would terrify them. To these people, you would be threatening their very existence as they know it.

When you are able to view the concept of prison in this way, then it becomes easier to have compassion with yourself for the prisons that you have constructed AND be compassionate towards others in the prisons they have built for themselves as well. The journey to peace can be a fully altering and sometimes radical experience than what you have become accustomed to experiencing in a dualistic world.

Let's talk about an example of a prison that we construct in our everyday lives. There is a woman who has had bad experiences with men from a young age. Perhaps, men have been violent towards her repeatedly. As a result, she does not like men. In fact, she has built a fortress around herself blocking any male energy from entering her safe house. Now, let's go back to the concept of oneness. If our reality (in Spirit) is that we are all united in one Spirit, then by blocking the male energy, the woman is really blocking herself to experience this oneness. She has imprisoned herself from experiencing her own truth and peace with her Creator and Source.

You might say, "Are we powerful enough to block ourselves from our Source?" The answer is yes. Our Source created us in his/her own image, and we are just as powerful. When we created duality, we created a place seemingly separate from God. We entered a dream state, but one that is very real to us because we built it. We have forgotten our true state of being. However, the good news is that we cannot be in this false state forever. It violates the rules of God, and therefore, the dream world of duality cannot last forever. Seemingly, one by one, we will all choose (at some point) to return home to him/her. We can only do this through forgiveness and eliminating the subconscious guilt buried deep inside due to our creation of the prison of duality.

Our forgiveness lessons in our lifetime become our way back home to our Source. As we ask Spirit to help us identify the prisons we have created, we can choose to release them. As our willingness to do this intensifies, we will feel freer and lighter in our bodies. The inner sense of peace will glow through us and attract others to make the same journey. Our prisons come in different forms, but they have all been manifested from the same unconscious guilt that created duality in the first place. Therefore, as we go about our separate journeys, we see (that in reality) we are all on the same path. This helps to eliminate judgment of ourselves and others. This helps us develop compassion for ourselves and others. When we have a moment of clarity and remember our truth, then we see this truth in everything surrounding us. Then, we are willing to work even harder at breaking down the obstacles that seemingly separate us from our Source.

CHAPTER 13

When all Else Fails, Remember Gratefulness

Gratefulness has been on my mind lately. It is easy to be grateful when life is going well, but harder when you're having a bad day.

Last week, one of my friends had an idea that a couple of us text each other three things we are grateful for every morning. Some days, the gratefulness flowed through my fingertips onto the text on the phone screen. Some days, I stared at my phone screen blankly. Not really sure what to type.

Sometimes we would type something very simple and other times it would be spiritually deep. But I am finding the exercise gratifying and helpful, especially on the days that don't go so well. Making myself type three things I am grateful for each morning (and sharing this with my friends) sets my course of thinking for the day. And, sometimes, finding even the smallest things to be grateful for, can reprogram negative thoughts and give me a more positive outlook.

We had a rough start this morning and I had to take Jack to St. Jude's Clinic. Normally, a day starting this way would put me in a bad mood and initiate anxious thought patterns. But, today, before Jack and I hit the road, I stopped and texted my three things that I am grateful for today. It not only stopped the anxious thoughts but placed me on a more peaceful mindset for the day. With the words of gratefulness washing over me, I felt empowered. As though typing those positive words and putting the message "out there," would transform my day.

Positivity is a mindset that can inspire uplifting change within yourself and it is contagious in a way that it positively influences others. I am grateful for the St. Jude's doctors and staff. I am grateful that Jack is reaching the end of cancer treatment. I am grateful for all of you. -Facebook post March 8, 2018

Early on, I noticed when I was in the midst of an uncontrollable scary situation, I always had control over the way I reacted to the situation. This did not come easily. Initially, the above situation would have brought me to tears, upset, and anger. Eventually, I learned to stop and take a deep breath. By doing this, I was interrupting any possible negative thought patterns and giving myself a reset. Then, I would search my mind for something.... anything where my focus could switch to gratefulness.

Jack's cancer treatment was a 3 ¼ year marathon, so I had several opportunities to practice. It did not come easily at first, but once I trained my mind to pause, that seemed to make a big difference. The pause allowed for space to move deep into my inner being. If I could not think of anything specific to be grateful for, then I would ask Spirit, "Okay, Pal, a little guidance here, please? Can you please help me see the silver lining on the cloud?" Then, I would stay still and quiet. Usually, a thought of gratefulness would come to mind. Sometimes, when a thought would not come to mind, I would just feel a wash of peace over me. Maybe the gratefulness in this situation was something that could not be expressed into words. Then, I would realize that I could be grateful for the fact that I am not alone on this journey, and guidance was given when I was willing to ask for it.

On another tough day during Jack's cancer treatment, when I was struggling with the concept of gratefulness, I posted the following:

> It is important to practice gratefulness (even in less than ideal circumstances), so here I go...
>
> I am grateful that Jack's fever broke last night.
>
> I am grateful that the hospital staff was able to find a cot for us last night. (This is really a big deal. Usually, one of us has to sleep on a couch and the other has to sleep in a hospital chair.) The cot was much more comfortable for my husband.
>
> I am grateful that Jack was able to go on his school field trip and celebrate his birthday before having to go to the hospital.
>
> I am grateful that we remembered to bring Jack's sheets (because he hates the smell of the hospital sheets).
>
> I am grateful that the hospital is not crowded, so Jack was given full attention by four nurses when we were admitted last night.
>
> I am grateful that the hospital staff gave Jack Tylenol last night to make him more comfortable (I cannot give him this at home because he cannot have it without being monitored by hospital staff).
>
> I am grateful for the kindness of the nurses, doctors, and staff.

I am grateful for a man who brought (much needed) coffee to our room this morning. Added bonus, he was thoughtful enough to chill the creamer on ice for us.

I am grateful for having an understanding workplace so I can be with my son when he is not feeling well.

I am grateful for healthy options on the hospital menu. The spinach, mushroom, and swiss omelet is pretty yummy.

I am grateful that Jack is out of bed and feeling well enough to play on his laptop this morning.

I am grateful for the sunshine pouring into our hospital window and for the beauty of the blossoming trees outside.

I am grateful for everyone's positive thoughts and prayers for Jack because we all need each other (and togetherness is so important).

With so much to be grateful for, I have everything I could possibly need right here, right now. As always, thanks for listening, everyone! -Facebook post May 7, 2018

In the above post, Jack had a nasty virus. Every time his fever would rise above 100.4 degrees, he would have to be admitted into the hospital. This was precautionary because he had a Mediport. Mediport's are amazing and cause less needle sticks for patients (i.e. once the Mediport is accessed, you can draw blood from it, and give all intravenous fluids and chemotherapy though it). It is way better than having several needle pricks to accomplish the same tasks. However, due to the risk of infection (it leads straight to the superior vena cava in the heart), if a fever rises above 100.4 degrees, the patient needs to be hospitalized. In addition, the patient will be immediately placed on antibiotics to attempt to kill off a possible infection in the Mediport (as a precaution). Most of the time, the fever is due to a virus or a bacterial infection; however, this procedure is always standard protocol due to the high risk of death if the patient has an infection in the Mediport.

We took many of these types of trips to the hospital. Some of them, I was able to handle with more grace than others. Sometimes, I would sulk and feel sorry for myself. Then, I would remember my inner work. Then, I would remember how useless and meaningless these helpless thoughts and mindsets were for me. Usually, I would regain my focus and attempt to turn it around. As I continued the inner work, and I continued to practice this new way of thinking, it became easier. More automatic. I didn't have to remind myself to practice it. Or, if I started the negative thinking train, I would catch myself more quickly and practice love and self-forgiveness with myself instead.

When I woke up at the hospital on this given morning, I asked Spirit to help me see the world around me without the blinders of my own lower-self conceived prejudices. Circumstantially, we were not in the best of situations; however, I asked that Spirit show me how to look through the circumstance at the light behind it. This asking resulted in the above Facebook post. I thought I would only be able to summon four to five lines of gratefulness, but the words of gratitude kept washing over me, and the words continued to spill out of my fingertips onto the phone screen. By the end of the post, I had written fourteen lines of gratefulness.

I learned a wonderful lesson on this day. How to find gratefulness in the seemingly mundane. How to take a not-so-great situation and see the blessings that were surrounding me. The blessings were always there. They are there for all of us. However, sometimes, we are so busy being grumpy with our circumstances that we do not allow the blessings to flow in or witness them when they are right in front of us. In fact, you might even say, we block the blessings from flowing in with our walls of bitterness and unhappiness.

Kate Richardson

Of course, the question is, "What about the death of a child? Would you be able to remain grateful in that situation?" I had to think about this often while Jack was going through cancer treatment. It was a serious situation with the potential of serious complications. I do not think I would succeed immediately at finding positivity, gratefulness, and forgiveness if any of my children passed away. I do not think it would be normal to breeze through such a situation without the natural process of grieving. However, I do know that I would need to eventually take steps to move forward towards forgiving the situation in the event it happened. Otherwise, I would be stuck in the same helpless trap of envisioning myself as the victim.

In the situation of a death of a loved one, it would be important to give myself the space to heal and allow my body to move through whatever process it needed to go through. If that means sobbing for hours, then I would sob for hours. If that means screaming at the top of my lungs, then I would scream at the top of my lungs. If that means breaking every dish in the house, then I would break every dish in the house. I believe denying the bodily states of grieving (especially early on) would be a sign of non-acceptance of the situation. Allowing the grief to move through you and past you is the only way that a person can ever really be free of it. I do not think it is something that would happen overnight, and I think this is a place where a person would need to endow themselves with the gifts of patience, love, and understanding. The important thing would be to decide (at some point, whenever you are ready) to move forward out of the darkness and despair of grief and learn to open the heart to love again. Not necessarily the love of another person but opening the heart to the unconditional love of divine Spirit. Allowing the love that the Universe provides to enter your heart and heal you. Being open to the idea of surrendering the pain, so it can be transformed to peace and acceptance.

Of course, when things are good, then we should rejoice and

bask in the goodness. Jack missed so many field trips and fun outings as a result of his cancer treatment. But he was healthy enough to enjoy his 6th grade field trip to the trampoline park. On this day, I posted:

> Just a quick line in gratefulness. So grateful that Jack was able to go on his 6th grade field trip to the trampoline park! Last year, he missed out on a field trip to Chicago because he was too sick to go. Love to hear the excitement in his voice as he describes the trampoline park. Love to see his exuberant smile. Love his appreciation for a trip with classmates where he jumped so much that he did nothing but drink big glasses of water when he came home. Jump high, Jack! You have come so far! And let the wind whisk you off to great new adventures! Fills my heart with happiness! -Facebook post May 4, 2018

Three days after I posted the above post, we were in the hospital (as mentioned in the gratefulness post earlier on). But Jack was NOT in the hospital on the day of the field trip, so that was a day to rejoice. I remember when he came home from school that day, he couldn't stop smiling. He was so excited to experience the normalcy of attending a field trip with peers. His positive energy and happiness were so contagious that I found myself smiling and bouncing on my toes as he told me all about the field trip. Gratefulness is not something to be practiced only on bad days. It is something to be practiced **every** day. Don't wait for a bad day to practice gratefulness. Practice it here and now wherever you are. Then, on the bad days, the gratefulness mindset will move through your thoughts more easily.

CHAPTER 14

And, Some Days, it just Takes Snow at the End of March

I would be lying to you if I told you I was filled with joy at the sight of the snow on the ground this morning. I begrudgingly went through my morning meditation asking for clarity and positivity.

I walked down the stairs, made my morning coffee, and looked through my patio window at my snowy backyard. I convinced myself this would not ruin my day, but be an opportunity instead.

Whether it be a bad day at work, crummy weather, or just an overall sense of listlessness, these all are important parts of our life journey. Sometimes while experiencing the harder times in life, we want to fight through it or resist what we are feeling at the time. Yet, when we surrender to how we feel at any given moment and acknowledge it (although we certainly do not have to enjoy it), sometimes we are able to move through the rough times more quickly.

With the snow on the ground at the end of March, I decided to practice this today. I walked outside and the cold wind took my breath away.

I told myself the fierce wind was reminding me to take a deep breath and find my inner calm. The cold rain and ice struck my face and hands. Although it stung, I told myself the rain and ice were awakening my soul and reminding me to never be complacent. When the ferocity of the wind pushed my body, I met the wind with my strength. I told myself the wind is a reminder that sometimes we need to access our inner strength in order to stay rooted to the earth when "life" tries to push us around.

No matter what the day brings, I am reminded that I am exactly where I need to be in order to learn life's lessons and fulfill my life's purpose. This is the same for all of you. Maybe today we will stay inside and do something we have intended to do for a long time, but never scheduled the time to do it. Paint a picture, write a poem, have a meaningful conversation with someone, cook your favorite meal, read a book. Do what fills you with joy and nourishes your soul, and you are on the right path.

If you are sad, surrender to the sadness and let it go. If you are angry, surrender to the anger and move past it. If you are happy, then rejoice and rest peacefully in your happiness. No matter where you are, you are exactly where you are supposed to be on your life's journey. So, don't be afraid to accept where you are today and know the light is never far away. -Facebook post March 24, 2018

On my time on Earth, surrender and acceptance are two of the biggest things in which I have struggled. Surrender does not mean to "give up," but to NOT "tense up." In other words, when something bad happens to me, I can feel the muscles in my body hardening. I am taking my emotions and reactions and physically pushing and storing them into my muscles. I may even develop a stomachache or a sore throat because I am associating the situation with "something bad" and choosing to hold the situation in my body. By doing this, I am making the situation a part of my identity. As the bad feelings involving the situation do not feel good, neither does deciding to hold these bad feelings inside my muscles, bones, and inner organs. So, when I say surrender, I am saying it is important to learn how to surrender and release these "bad feelings," so that we can be free of the effects they have on the mind and the body.

For example, approximately one year after Jack's cancer treatment, I was having a terrible pain in my lower abdomen. The pain had gradually become worse and worse until it reached a pinnacle of the worst pain I have felt in my life. Ironically, the pain I suffered manifested in the same way my son's cancer diagnosis manifested. I had pain in the abdomen and lower back, and there was pressure in my sacrum when I sat upright in a chair. My son's symptoms were eerily similar in his cancer diagnosis.

Many doctor's visits later, I learned my uterus was enlarged, contained inflammation and some abnormal cells, and needed to be removed. This diagnosis was a major sign to me that I needed to surrender and release the pain and suffering I endured as a mother of a child with a cancer diagnosis. It became evident to me that I needed to create more space in my life for healing and that self-care was paramount in this process. I began to remove unnecessary obligations in my life, and I chose to make space for self-healing. I began to surround myself with positive people who were willing to support me on my journey. I began to integrate a stronger yoga practice and eat healthier. I relentlessly did my morning and evening meditations in addition to my daily

Reiki self-healing practices. I began these integrative practices to heal my insides which included my mind and my body.

The space I created for myself along with my healing practices were important for two reasons. For one, it allowed me to accept the fact that I do not need to be Wonder Woman and the epitome of strength and power that she embodies in my present state. It is okay for me to be where I am in this moment, and I was not feeling like Wonder Woman at this time. I am a person who went through a traumatic event, and I need to care for myself just as much as I would care for another human being suffering a similar event. At the moment, I was broken, but I had an opportunity to fix myself. This process of accepting the fact that I was involved in something traumatic was salient because it pulled me out of a state of busyness and denial. Formerly, I was attempting to keep busy helping others so that I could deny the pain I felt inside as a result of my son's cancer diagnosis. I was running from the pain. Accepting that I needed self-care and self-love was the first part of the healing process. Once I could accept the fact that I was still suffering from residual pain that I had never processed, I could surrender and choose to release the pain.

Surrender can happen in different ways for everyone. For me, surrendering came the most natural to me during meditation. I would begin by doing a scan of my body and notice where I was holding tension. I would pay special attention to any physical discomfort or pain I may have been feeling at the time. Then, I would pay attention to my breath, and take normal, even inhales and exhales. This process would help me to quiet the inner brain chatter so that I could tap-in to my Source or Spirit.

Then, I would simply ask, "Can you help me release my inner pain and suffering?" Usually, a past thought would come to mind that I had not forgiven. Sometimes, this thought would relate to Jack's cancer treatment, and sometimes it would be something entirely different. As the thought came to my mind, I focused

91

on breathing through the thought. I tried to remember that this past thought was haunting me because I refused to let go of the pain it caused me. I was making an identity out of the pain and choosing to hold onto it. Then, I would say something like, "I lovingly release this past memory. I lift it to Spirit, and I allow it to move through me and past me. I choose to disengage from the labels I have placed on this memory, so I can release it fully." Sometimes, the same "bad memory" would recur during different meditations. I would remind myself to not be frustrated by this, but to move towards forgiving the thought again and again if necessary. I knew that my determination towards letting go of this pain would ultimately allow me to release it fully and finally.

How did I know if I was successful in eradicating a painful memory? I could tell if I had truly let go and forgiven a situation when I could look on the memory and no longer feel the pain associated with it. Usually, if I was carrying this pain in a part of my body, then the pain would subside. Sometimes, I would just notice a lightness of the body, as though something heavy had been lifted off it. These were all signs that I had successfully released and forgiven sections of my painful past.

During this process of healing, I realized that becoming Wonder Woman was a little different than the comic books. Becoming Wonder Woman was learning to accept a situation as it is in the present moment and learning to surrender and let go of past pain. Becoming Wonder Woman is recognizing the "faults" I may have in order to overcome them. Becoming Wonder Woman is learning to be comfortable in my own skin and allowing myself to be vulnerable. Becoming Wonder Woman is learning to trust that I am enough when I feel alone.

Acceptance is experiencing a situation that you have no control over on this Earth and letting go of any resistance to the situation. When you resist a terrible situation, you are creating more pain, and usually end up holding this pain in the body. One of the greatest lessons we can learn together is to learn to accept (not necessarily like) whatever situation we are experiencing in the present moment. If we can learn to accomplish this goal, then we will be able to move through challenging situations more easily and fluidly. We don't have to like the situation, but we can choose to accept the present moment. Then, we can evaluate whether or not there is something we can actionably do to improve the situation. If there is an action we can take to help, great! If the situation is entirely out of our control (as was the case with Jack's cancer treatment), then accept. The acceptance will allow us to make better decisions in these circumstances and move us towards a state of healing. The lack of resistance will allow the pain to move through the body instead of lodging itself somewhere in the nooks and crannies of our being.

Surrender implies letting go of this concept of control. Sometimes, we feel safer when we feel like we have control over a given situation. However, there are many life situations that we have no control over. Placing yourself in a state of surrender is NOT giving up on life. Placing yourself in a state of surrender implies taking these big, tough circumstances and surrendering them to a Higher Power. To trust there is a Higher Power that is taking care of your needs no matter how horrible your situation may seem at the time. To surrender is to learn to release the pain you are experiencing to Spirit, so it can be lifted from you. Acceptance and surrender are both key components on the path to becoming your true, best self.

CHAPTER 15

Surviving Versus Thriving

As I went on a walk today, I noticed the many dandelion flowers polka-dotted across the green grass in the fields. I was enjoying looking at the stark contrast between the lush green grass and the feathery yellow flowers. It was like stars glistening across the night sky in earth form. It held a beauty of its own.

But the truth is, the dandelion is not humanity's favorite flower. The human psyche subconsciously wants to eradicate this golden flower from their yards and landscapes. And I wondered why? The dandelion is not an ugly flower. It is rich in vitamins A, C, and K, and is a good source of calcium, potassium, iron, and manganese; therefore, it can be used to nourish our bodies. It flourishes and can grow anywhere.

And, that is when it dawned on me. The dandelion is a survivor. It can survive through hot and cold temperatures and can grow in virtually any type of soil. They can grow in the sun or in the shade. When the lawnmower mows them down, they adapt and grow shorter stalks, so the mower will not cut them down a second time. Undoubtedly, they are the garden variety of the cockroach. They seem to survive almost anything you throw at them.

Although there is a time in life to survive, it is unhealthy to live in this mode indefinitely. To barely make it by, to survive in the cold when you could thrive in the sun. Hanging by our pinky fingers on the bottom rung of a ladder and telling ourselves, "It's okay. I'm making it. I haven't fallen yet. I'm a survivor."

Sometimes, we applaud ourselves for being "survivors," but is this really any way to live? Eventually those pinky fingers will wear out from fatigue and you need to have a solid earth foundation to land upon when this happens. Or, better yet, as you are dangling from the bottom rung of the ladder, you reach out from within and make steps to thrive instead of just survive. You begin reaching up and climbing back up the ladder (slowly and steadily) one rung at a time.

So, maybe the dandelion reminds us that we are all survivors in one manner or another. And, sometimes this reminder can be painful (therefore, the subconscious urge to remove them from our presence). When we walk past a dandelion growing in the crack in the sidewalk, it reminds us that it is surviving, but not thriving. It reminds us that we may be living stagnant between a rock and a hard place and not giving ourselves the room we need to blossom fully. When we see a dandelion with a short stalk, we are reminded the dandelion grew smaller as a defense mechanism in order to survive. It was cut down and grew back quieter/closer to the ground in order to be quietly present in this life, but not be heard.

Our lives can reflect the survival instinct of the dandelion. When we do not allow for space in our lives, we place ourselves in that crack in the sidewalk. We do not give ourselves the room needed to flourish. When we are cut down by the words of another person, we may cower and retreat low to the ground as a defense. We may choose to close ourselves off from other people for fear of being hurt again. We may become a smaller version of our true selves.

With Jack's cancer treatment coming to a close in August, I realize that (as a family), we have mostly been just surviving. We have learned the ways of the dandelion. We have made it through some very painful moments over the last three years, and we have done what we have needed to do to survive the traumatic experiences. At the end of Jack's cancer treatment in August, it is my hope that we can break this cycle of "surviving" and allow the future to mushroom into a whole new life experience.

It is my hope that we will learn steady gratefulness, to live life fully, to let go of fear and anxiety, to move into a whole new realm of exciting new possibilities. To try new things, to give ourselves space to grow, to remember to give Jack independence so that he has space to grow as well. This will be my goal as we near the end of this chapter. To teach myself the importance of boldly expanding my horizons and not allowing fear, rejection, and worry to stifle my growth.

Yes, I am very grateful that Jack will be a cancer survivor, but I do not want him to hold onto this title as a crutch. I want this experience to be a part of his life journey, but I do not want this to be his identity. I want him to be a former cancer patient that has learned to thrive. I want the disease to be a distant memory that was the catalyst for positive change in our lives. Just another part of our story. I want Jack to be so full of life and joy and happiness that it pours over into the people around him. I want this healing for our whole family.

Ahhhh, the dandelion. When we come to the moment of the next new chapter in our lives, I will look at you and remember your lessons well. You showed us how to survive in the tiniest of spaces, you showed us how to shiver to survive the cold, and you showed us how to derive nutrients out of the poorest of soils for food for our bodies. For this, we are grateful. But now it is time to turn to a new teacher for lessons. Lessons that will assist us in moving past survival mode and learning how to prosper. -Facebook post April 25, 2018

My husband I and like to eat at a local restaurant in town where they have a **sommelier** on staff. We do not buy expensive wines, but sometimes it is fun to find a 20-dollar bottle to bring home after we eat dinner. As we were purchasing our wine at the register, I mentioned to the sommelier that we had recently returned from a wine trip in Southern Illinois with friends. The sommelier scoffed at the idea of the Illinois wines, so I asked him why. He said a Norton grape or a Chambourcin grape grown in Illinois will always taste the same. He said it would always taste the same because the soil is **too** good for growing crops in Illinois, so the wines lack depth and unique properties.

The grape vines grow too easily because they have all the things they need readily available to them for survival.

He further explained the best tasting wines come from areas where the grape vines are forced to struggle. In arid areas in the sides of a mountain where the roots must reach deep into the rocky crags in order to pull the nutrients and water out of the soil are the best places to grow grape vines. In their quest for survival, the grape vines grown in these areas dig deep and absorb the property of the soils around them causing them to have more unique qualities and depth of flavor. That is why some of these wines will taste like violets, have earthy qualities, or taste like minerals prevalent in the soil in which they are grown. It gives these wines a complexity and flavor that wine lovers readily enjoy.

Just as the grape vines who endure the struggles for survival produce the best wines, humans also grow and develop better traits through their trying times and forgiveness lessons during their lifetimes. In our lives, there is a time for both. During Jack's cancer treatment, we were barely making it as a family day by day. Sometimes, just scraping by. We were most definitely just surviving. When one person was having a particularly difficult day, another person in the family would try to be the "strong" person to lift the other one up. However, there were times when we were all having a tough day. On these days, we each individually had to dig deep into our being to help move us through the day. We had to pull ourselves through the thick mud our minds were treading through in order to survive another day. We all had our different ways of handling these moments in order to pull ourselves out of the muck.

After Jack's cancer treatment was completed, we had to learn to move forward. To peel back the layers and habits we developed to survive in order to make headway in the realm of thriving. Sometimes, it was very easy to fall into old thought patterns. When Jack would complain that he did not feel well, my heart would start beating loudly in my chest. My mind would run me through a list of possible ailments, and there was always the fear of relapse in the back of my mind. Gradually, I had to convince myself (and eventually fully believe) that his cancer would not return. If it ever did, then I would have to deal with it and learn to accept the situation. But, in the present moment, I had to treat him like a normal, healthy child. I had to consider the normal level of possibilities for his discomfort before jumping to irrational conclusions. I needed to believe that everything was going to be exactly as it should be. Maybe not the way I would have planned, but exactly as it should be in order to build each one of us up into our best possible selves.

Learning to thrive included shedding old fears and anxieties and allowing each one of us (as a family) to just be. It included looking at the gifts given to us in this lifetime by Spirit and allowing these gifts to manifest and develop into their fullest potential. For my husband and son, their creativity took form in the manifestation of physical objects. Both my husband and son love to build and construct. They both especially enjoy cars and learning more about the construction regarding them. They enjoy taking a car and adding their own style and exuberance to a dull, old-school manufactured frame.

Learning to thrive for them meant expressing their creativity in this form. They would let go of fear and anxiety in the world where perfectionism is valued, and, instead, experiment with this form of creativity. This was an important process in letting go of past pain, fear, and anxiety regarding Jack's cancer treatment as well. Developing confidence in building something new built their inner character. With this confidence, it became easier to release fear and anxiety. When you are building something new, there is the fear and anxiety that you may not "get it right." In Jack's cancer treatment, there was fear and anxiety over the uncertainties taking place in his body. The form just changed (working on a car/cancer treatment), but not what needed to be released. Whether he let go of fear and anxiety regarding working on the car or let go of fear and anxiety regarding his cancer treatment, it is all the same. By overcoming fear and anxiety in one situation, he can learn to overcome the same fear and anxiety in another situation. In both situations, Jack had the opportunity to release fear and anxiety. He had an opportunity to overcome both regardless of the form it took. To step into his power and learn to thrive. I found when Jack and my husband were expressing themselves in this way, they were happier, less anxious, and more prosperous. They were taking important steps towards thriving.

Learning to thrive for me meant the undoing of past negative thought patterns. The gift given to me by Spirit had always been writing. Although I have always found it difficult to express myself verbally to another person, I have always found it much easier to express myself through written form. During Jack's treatment, I started the process of writing through my Facebook posts. It gave me an outlet for expressing my thoughts and feelings to the Universe. At first, it was difficult for me because I worried about judgment from others and it was extremely vulnerable for me to discuss my deepest soul- searching thoughts with the Facebook world. Some of my Facebook friends were close friends, but some of them were people who cared deeply about Jack and wanted updates on his treatment. Therefore, I did not have close associations with every one of my Facebook friends. So, I was sharing my soul stories with some complete strangers. This made me feel extremely vulnerable, but I knew it was a salient part of my healing process, so I continued to post my thoughts and feelings anyway.

Through this writing process, I began the process of sorting through my past negative thought patterns and transmuting them into positive thought patterns instead. Through my own writing, Spirit taught me to be kind to myself, to be grateful for others, and to trust that the Universe was looking out for me and my family. Through this creative process, I found my voice. By speaking my thoughts through written form, I was able to whittle through my busy mind and weed out what was needed for me in my healing process.

We are on a continual path as a family to keep moving forward on this path to thriving. We work hard to allow ourselves the space and freedom to be our true selves. We constantly try to remember the importance of staying true to our purpose. We are on a constant quest to follow our own rules despite the social norm. Our rules, of course, include what divine guidance would impart to us in this lifetime. For example, current social norms trend towards people being "perfect" in every way. Perfect bodies, perfect jobs, perfect homes, perfect cars. But being "perfect" is being exactly as God created you. Not being like everyone else on the planet. A person could have very little materially, yet be blissful in the knowledge he or she contains about the Universe.

Thriving is not creating a false temple around yourself but freeing yourself from all past social norms which fed your fears and anxiety in the first place. Thriving is learning to give yourself the freedom to be YOU (your Higher Self) without any pretense or fear of judgment from others. We are enveloped by several titles while we inhabit a body: mother, father, friend, accountant, pilot, yogi, helper, fixer, enemy, thief, murderer. The list goes on and on. Some would say these titles are a part of your identity. They would say the different roles you play help facilitate societal structure in a world of duality. In reality, these titles are just a form of separation. A distraction keeping you from remembering your true self. We become so busy trying to "live up" to our titles that we forget our true purpose.

If every person on the planet could learn to free themselves from what society says they should be, and instead, just be exactly as their Source created them, then the world would be a much more beautiful place. If every person could embrace their gifts and true purpose in this world without the constraints of the false importance placed on material items and the need to be special and separate from others, then every person in this world would be free. This is the definition of thriving. Freedom from what the world says is important for you to have and knowing that you already have everything you need within yourself. There is nothing in the outside world that would make you thrive, the ability to thrive already lies within yourself. The Universe placed this light in you long ago and it is still there ready for you to access it. Expressing yourself through your creativity (in whichever form it may take in this place and time) is paramount. The freedom to be you without the need for false pretenses. To just be as you are and allow the light to move through you for your life's purpose. If everyone on the planet could fully embrace their true, Higher Self, then the entire planet would be healed. This, my friends, is thriving.

CHAPTER 16

Making Way for New Growth

I have a planting with gorgeous purple leaves at the corner of my driveway with an impressively large weed growing out of it. I have been battling the weed for three years now. I cut large portions of the weed out of the shrub (trying not to cut too deep for fear of harming the bush along with the weed). Yet, no matter how hard I try to eliminate this weed's grasp on my precious shrub, it grows back more quickly and larger than ever before. As usual, nature is trying to tell me something.

The weed has tightly wound itself around the root system of my plant and refuses to let go. The weed has become so much a part of the plant, I cannot kill the weed without destroying the plant as well. I know this is the case, but I keep peeling away layers of weed, hoping to get a different result than the time before. But the weed keeps winning.

It is readily apparent that I need to remove both the weed and the plant. That is the only way. But I really love the purple leaves on my plant and the way its branches raise and then slope downward touching the earth. I like the way it gently blows in the wind and caresses the ground with the leaves at the end of its branches. I am attached to the brightness and beauty in the plant. The plant represents the self, the one I have always known and have grown comfortable with.

Just as a weed can integrate itself with a plant's root system, there are similar things in our lives that become attached to us. Usually, these are situations and negative thought patterns that we would do better without. But sometimes we have carried them for so long, we forget where our bodies end and the weed begins. Eventually, we might name the thing that is no longer needed in our lives, and we peel layers away a little at a time (knowing damn good and well that it is tightly wrapped around our root system and will eventually pop up again). But we convince ourselves that we are making progress.

Sometimes it is necessary to remove the plant along with the weed. It is a scary thing to do because the plant is part of our identity. It is who we think we are. If we destroy the plant along with the weed, we may have to start over. We may have to experience a rebirth. We may have to make some major life changes. But, when the deep-seated thoughts or life situations that no longer serve us need to be evaluated for change and renewal, sometimes a renewal of the self is in order as well.

And, this doesn't have to be scary. It can be an exciting new adventure which brings a person closer to their truth and their passions. The rebirth that comes from the ashes of old ideas can be the most profound and precious. Sometimes, finding the courage to let go of the "old self" can be difficult. It comes with the worry, "If I let go of something that big, will I still exist?" It becomes easy to be complacent with "the known" for fear of the unknown. If I remove the plant along with the weed, what will grow back in its place? The fear is that the new growth will be another weed. Maybe one that strangles the life out of you this time.

When confronted with this type of situation, trust becomes paramount. Learning to trust in a Higher Power. Learning to trust in the support of others around you. Learning that you can exist as something much greater than you originally imagined. Releasing fear and anxiety and coming to the realization that there is a bigger, unseen possibility. By eliminated broken relationships, negative self-talk, and limiting beliefs you can grow into something more beautiful than you can possibly imagine. And, knowing that you don't have to be alone on the journey. -Facebook post October 28, 2018

As we progress through life, we begin to identify those thought patterns that work for us and those thought patterns that work against us. In fact, in our human lifetime, we often encounter many changes in the ways in which we process thoughts as our experiences continue to advance. The grief that comes from some of our traumatic experiences can become an eye-opener to some of the deep-seated bad habits we have embedded in our psyche.

There is a natural tendency to cling to old belief systems because we have usually built an identity around a particular thought system that may have been helpful in the past. However, in order to grow, we must eliminate the old thought system all together and reconstruct a new way of thinking.

In my healing process, one of the larger negative thought patterns I identified with was scarcity. Every spring, a large bush in our back yard would grow berries that the birds in the neighborhood adored. For three consecutive years, I noticed a robin who would stand watch over this bush in anticipation of the growth of the berries in early spring. When another bird would fly to the bush, the robin would quickly chase it away. Once the berries grew on the tree, the robin would become particularly vicious with the other birds, chirping and swooping down on the other birds in an attempt to intimidate them out of the bush. However, there was a multitude of berries on the tree which could easily have fed many birds. Yet, the robin hovered and protected the bush as though his survival depended on it, and he refused to share them with the other birds. At the end of the spring, the robin would sit under the bush, so fat with the berries he had eaten that he could barely walk or fly. He sat there swollen with his feathers in disarray because they could no longer lay flat against his body. His scarcity instinct left him bloated, uncomfortable, and alone beneath the bush.

This robin was acting in the survival mindset. He did not trust a Higher Power to lead him to other bushes once the berries were gone. In his survival mindset, his food needs were met; however, his relationships with the other birds suffered. Even though his nutritional needs were met, he ate more than his body needed in his refusal to share the berries with the other birds. Even though he was fed, his body became large preventing him from flying to other bushes to find other sources of food. Not only was the robin blocking his own needs through overeating, but he isolated himself from the companionship of the other birds through his attack. And he made it difficult for himself to locate another food source once the bush was bare of sustenance by becoming overweight and bloated. It was obvious that the extra weight made it more difficult for the robin to move. Although the robin was not starving his body, he was starving his soul.

If the robin would have acted in a thriving mindset, he would have found that his needs could have been met more easily. By not anxiously chasing away the other birds, he may have been able to follow them to other food sources once the food was depleted. By choosing to live harmoniously with the other life forms around him, he would have only eaten what his body needed, and he would not have become too fat to move. By trusting the Universe to provide for him, he would have developed instincts which would have guided him to his next source of nutrition.

So, when I say, sometimes you must remove the plant along with the weed, I am not suggesting you destroy yourself. What I am saying is you may have to tear down old, worn-out belief systems in exchange for a new perspective. The reason this can be so difficult is because the old thought systems might have been helpful in the past. We might think, "Well, it worked before. Why isn't it working now?"

The answer is these old thought patterns might have helped move you through a situation where you were just surviving; however, these same thought patterns cannot move you towards thriving. Thriving takes a new perspective in thought and a heap of trust towards a Higher Power in believing that your needs will be met. These needs may not be met the way you think they should be, but they will be met for your highest and best good as needed for your particular life journey.

If you are at a point in your journey where the old ways are no longer working, then I would suggest moving into a state of "no mind." Letting go of the busyness of the mind through meditation, a run in the woods, yoga... whatever works best for you. Ask your spirit guides to remove the obstacles created by survival thinking so you can move forward with thriving thinking. Survival thinking is scarcity. It is just getting by. Thriving thinking is new creation and growth. It is living life with joy, peace, and in alignment with your truest and best Higher Self. When you learn to operate through the process of thriving thinking, then anything is possible. You can manifest miracles in the world around you because you are in alignment with your Source. You are trusting those base needs will be met because you are fulfilling your life purpose on this Earth. Therefore, you no longer need to operate under survival thinking. You have made the decision to move past this level of thinking to a higher level of thinking. Under the thriving level of thinking, the sky is the limit. You will find yourself happier, lighter, and more serene. You will be living your life joyfully. Trusting that a Higher Power can see the bigger picture, so you can focus on thriving thinking which includes the knowledge that this Higher Power will guide you to the next food source once one has been depleted. This includes giving yourself room to focus on your growth.

My biggest obstacle towards thriving thinking was not giving myself the space needed to grow. I was filling my life with busyness, so that I could not focus on my internal growth. Even seemingly good practices can get in the way of your thriving thinking and growth. Yoga is an excellent way to benefit the body and mind. However, if you had a particularly busy day, maybe meditation or an epsom salt bath would give you the same body and mind rejuvenation. If you are doing anything (even seemingly positive things) to excess, you can lose yourself in these things and miss the bigger picture. Don't get stuck in a rut. Give yourself room to grow and be open to switching it up as you are guided to do so. If we can move away from survival thinking and towards thriving thinking, then we will benefit indefinitely. Not only will we be benefitting ourselves, but we will be in a place where we are able to benefit others as well.

CHAPTER 17

Trusting Your Gut

Today was Jack's second to last intravenous chemotherapy treatment. Yay! His last one is on August 13. He was scheduled to have a spinal chemotherapy on top of his usual intravenous vincristine in August. After the troubles we had with the last one, I strongly feel that his body is saying, "I have had enough of these things. They are no longer necessary. I want to heal." So, I knew I was going to have a conversation with the oncologist today. I thought I might be met with opposition, but I felt compelled to have the conversation anyway. The conversation went something like this...

Me: I would like to have a discussion with you regarding Jack's last spinal chemotherapy in August. We have decided, as a family, that we want to opt out of it.

Doctor: Why do you want to opt out of it?

Me: Well, for starters, there were many complications with the last one he had in May which caused him a lot of discomfort and pain. And, I feel like that was his body telling us it is time to stop. I understand that you are a doctor and depend on science and research data to make decisions. I am a police officer and I trust my gut instincts and intuition. So, I try to meet you in the middle. But the bottom line is I do not feel it is necessary or will have any bearing on the possibility of a relapse. I do not think the cancer is going to return either way. So, I just don't want to put him through that trauma anymore.

Doctor: I agree. At this point in treatment, I don't think it would make a difference.

She spoke with his primary oncologist and she agreed to cancel the spinal chemo in August. He still will have the intravenous vincristine and oral chemo, but those spinal chemotherapy procedures are really not fun (so, I am very relieved he will not have to endure another one).

I am happy that the doctors listened to me and were not resistant to the idea. Even the nurses I spoke to today had the same feeling. One nurse said, "Yeah. I don't think I would want to do another one after what happened last time. I just don't think it is necessary." I take this collective experience as a sign that we made the right choice as a family. It surprised me a little, but everyone was on board and had the same thoughts. No resistance at all.

And, I am very excited to say, only one more chemo treatment left! -Facebook post July 18, 2018

What do you do if you feel Spirit is guiding you to do something that is not in alignment with worldly principles and social norms? Begin taking steps in that general direction and see what happens. There have been times when I thought I was being guided by Spirit to do something only to later find it was something my lower self (survival thinking) wanted. Our lower selves (or egos) can be tricky sometimes, and the ego can disguise and entertain certain ideas to distract you and prevent your growth. Remember, old habits die hard. It's hard to remove the ego from the picture when it comes to deciding what is best for us. After all, we think, "I should know what is best for myself." However, when you trust a Higher Power to decide what is best for you, you can never go wrong. A Higher Power does not have the narrow scope of knowledge you possess in any given situation because this Higher Power is not stuck in a body. A Higher Power can see the entire picture and impart the wisdom it sees to you from its much larger perspective. A Higher Power transcends space and time which makes this possible.

In the above post, I decided to take steps towards disallowing Jack's final intrathecal chemotherapy treatment. I knew that if this was the wrong decision, there would be signs and obstacles motivating me to make another decision. But if it was the right decision, the guidance to take this action would be obvious. There would be less obstacles and the situation would go more smoothly.

When I wake up in the morning, I always ask, "Spirit guides, please guide me truly. And help me distinguish the difference between the thinking of my lower self and the thinking of my higher self." If I begin taking steps towards guidance I am given, Spirit-guided (thriving thinking) ideas will usually positively encourage me to keep moving in that direction. If I begin taking steps towards guidance I am given, and I am being confronted with constant obstacles, then I might rethink it. Maybe it was a divinely guided idea, but the time is not right. Or, maybe my lower self is disguising itself in sheep's clothing to distract me from spiritual growth. It is not always easy to distinguish between the two, so I ask for guidance in discerning the best path for me. I have found the ultimate difference between the two can be quite simple if I can get in touch with my emotions. How does the idea make me feel? I will ask myself this question after meditating on it. If the idea carries any weight of anxiety or fear, then it is usually an idea from my lower self (ego). If the idea gives me excitement, peace, or joy, then it is usually an idea from my higher self (Spirit). It takes time and effort, but if you keep practicing this, then you will learn to trust the voice of your higher self.

It can be difficult to follow spiritual guidance, especially if it defies social norms. When I had the discussion with Jack's oncologist about eliminating his last spinal chemotherapy treatment, I worried about judgment.

Judgment from other mothers, "What is she thinking? Does she want to risk her son falling into a relapse? I would NEVER do that!"

Judgment from the doctors, "We are the professionals here. Why is she questioning us?"

And judgment from myself, "What if I cancel the last spinal chemotherapy and Jack's cancer relapses? Can I live with that? Or will I blame myself for making this decision?"

Since this was an emotionally charged decision, I decided to take baby steps towards it and see what happened. I decided if there was great resistance from the medical staff or if I didn't feel at peace as I was having the conversation with the medical staff, then I would abort the idea.

However, once I started talking to the doctor about it, I felt myself transitioning to autopilot. As though Spirit was helping me with the right words to express how I felt about the situation. I felt at peace throughout the entire conversation with the medical staff, and they responded in kind. That is how I knew the above decision was the right one to make regarding Jack's medical treatment. It was an idea, once furthered, that was coated in a layer of peace and understanding. The truth of the idea resonated throughout the doctor's office. And when the truth reached the ears of the doctors and nurses, I think they could feel the peace behind it too. That is what a Spirit-led idea feels like.

Conversely, ego or lower self-led thinking has a different feeling. For example, I had an idea to go back to school to obtain a massage therapy degree, so I could help relieve suffering for others. After watching my son progress through cancer treatment, I thought this was the perfect way for me to "give back" to society. The process of going back to school at the age of 41 was daunting, but I pushed through the process anyway. At every turn, there was obstacle after obstacle. Yet, I kept pushing through, determined that I was going to help others with this idea, and it was something I was supposed to do. I took a difficult human anatomy prerequisite class that took away time from home. When I was home, I was studying all the time. I was stressed out, gaining weight, and the opposite of being at peace. Yet, I ignored what I was feeling because I wanted to help others, and I was convinced this was the best way to do it. Obstacles kept popping up, and I ignored the signs and kept aggressively pushing through. My ego said, "I made this commitment and I am going to follow through come hell or high water." With very little ease, I was finally accepted into the massage therapy program. I was happy. Finally, I will be able to help others, I thought.

I never stopped to meditate on it or ask Spirit for advice, I just kept pushing through. And, if I did ask for advice from Spirit, and I didn't like what Spirit said, I would manipulate the meaning to fit this desire that I had. It wasn't until I had a medical issue pop up the day before the massage therapy classes began that I finally took the hint. I needed to stop and heal myself before I could heal others. My busyness with classes and studying was preventing me from going deep within and healing past traumas that desperately needed to be dealt with and released. And Spirit said, "Finally! I thought you were never going to get it."

Although I was upset at first, I realized I had been moving forward with this idea from lower self-led thinking. Not to say I couldn't be a massage therapist sometime in the future, but the time was not right. There was inner work to be done. Within a day, I felt at peace with the decision to drop the massage therapy program and focus on my own physical, emotional, and spiritual health instead. This peace (which I never felt while moving towards the massage therapy goal) told me that I was making the right decision to drop the program.

The ego was cunning on that idea, "But you will be helping others. Isn't it worth sacrificing your own healing for a while so you can help others?" The reality is that I cannot help others without healing myself first. Spirit had been gently placing obstacles in my way to give me guidance, but I was ignoring it. It was a good lesson in discernment. Moving into the future, I am learning to pay better attention to the signs and feelings surrounding a situation or idea. The ego can cleverly convince you with logic that its ideas are sound; however, it cannot surround the idea with peace. Only Spirit can surround the idea with peace because it is the truth. That is how you can tell the difference. Learn to trust your feelings. Learn to focus and discern between the two. Learn to let go of an idea if it is not moving towards your best interests. This does not always come easily. Keep practicing and be vigilant!

CHAPTER 18

Stepping Outside of Your Comfort Zone

Mini vacation at Holiday World in Santa Claus, Indiana. Friday and Saturday, we fiercely rode thrilling water rides and roller coasters until we were sore and tired. On Sunday morning, we walked around the property at Santa's Cottages to pose for a couple of pictures and play on the playground.

But, of course, I have a story to share...

On Saturday, we were in line for a water roller coaster called the Monsoon. It was crowded, so the lifeguards were filling the boats with 5 or 6 people. When Jack realized we would have to share our intimate boat ride with a stranger, he threatened to not ride at all. (Oh my God, what if we have to touch feet!) You see, after everything he has gone through at a young age, Jack doesn't feel safe. So, sometimes new people and new experiences can cause a heap of anxiety. And, if I am honest with myself, I have always been the same way. So, I can relate. There are times when I would be very content just holing up in my house for a week with very little human contact at all.

And, can you blame us? Sometimes people can be scary and commit atrocious acts of violence. I can hardly stand to watch the news anymore. I don't want to be exposed to the terrible things we do to one another on a daily basis. I don't want to let down my guard and be vulnerable. Some days, I want to place an invisible force field around myself to keep everyone out. Because when humanity is not committing acts of physical violence, they are still committing acts of emotional violence which is just as isolating and disturbing. Hateful words, shunning one another because of differing viewpoints, and neglecting one another's cries for help and belonging.

So, when Jack said he didn't want to ride the ride with a stranger, I understood how he felt. But, sometimes, being fierce is more than being brave enough to ride a roller coaster. Sometimes being fierce is allowing yourself to be vulnerable to interactions with strangers. To trust that regardless of the type of interaction you encounter, that we all really want the same thing. To be included, to belong, to be loved. And, if the encounter is negative, and you can respond with compassion instead of anger, then this is one of the most heroic and brave deeds that you can accomplish.

So, I tell Jack that he may get to sit by a cute girl on the ride, and we should just trust that it will all work out. When it was our turn, the single rider that was placed in our group was a large man in his late 50's. Trying to muster up all the courage I could, I turned to the man and said,

"Hello. Have you ever ridden this ride before?" He replied, "Sure. Everyday." I wasn't sure I heard him right. I asked, "Everyday?" He explained to me that he lived in the area and had a season pass to the theme park. He wasn't there with family, he was there alone. And, he had the courage to ride these rides daily with complete strangers. To allow himself to be vulnerable in a way that would be very difficult for me to do.

The good news is my initial interaction with the man soon became contagious for my whole family. When Jack saw that I had the courage to engage a stranger, it gave him the courage to do the same. Pretty soon, Jack was asking him about his favorite rides at the park. Our daughter, Emma, sat next to him in the boat. We laughed and screamed on the ride with our new, temporary member of our family. And, when the man had problems exiting the boat at the end of the ride, my husband stayed behind to reach out his hand and assist him.

It is a small thing, but huge to me. I feel like amidst all the thrill rides at the park, this is the bravest thing we did that day as a family. Engaging a stranger with kindness and letting go of the anxiety and fear that sometimes accompanies these encounters. Usually, we would shy away from this type of experience for fear of rejection or getting hurt. We made ourselves just a little vulnerable and trusted it would be safe. To extend love and belonging to a man who ventured daily to a water park by himself. To make him a part of our family for even just a small part of the day. -Facebook post July 16, 2018

*T*here were many situations regarding Jack's cancer treatment that forced me to step out of my comfort zone. My personality definitely falls into the introvert category. I like my alone time. I am not a fan of small talk. I am a few, small-number-of-friends type of person rather than a many- acquaintances-and-friends type of person. And although I have always cared for others, I rarely (if ever) would engage strangers unless deemed necessary. If I witnessed a stranger drop something, I would catch their attention and let them know. But I never started a conversation with them. And if the person attempted to start a conversation with me, I would awkwardly just smile and nod my head. Like I said, I am not good at small talk. For me, it takes a heap of energy to engage another person. Therefore, if I am going to expend that energy, then I am going to trend towards meaningful conversation. I am going to ask personal questions. I am probably going to hit on some philosophical or metaphysical topics. And if you are a complete stranger to me, then chances are, I will make you uncomfortable by being so personal. Ah, the life and complexities of an introvert.

At the cancer clinic, we were the family that mostly kept to ourselves. The most I could muster on most days was to give other families reassuring smiles or a nod of the head. It was such a painful experience to not only watch my own child go through the perils of cancer treatment, but to watch other children and families go through the same trauma. As a coping mechanism, I used to practice looking at the children who were suffering and try to look past the pain to see the light within them instead. I did the same with the parents, especially the ones having a particularly bad day. Since it was hard for me to engage strangers, I decided I could still send the families my prayers and blessings in this way. I could tell by the looks on some of their faces that it sometimes helped. If I could look on a suffering child and see the wholeness of God in them, then I knew I had a look of awe and adoration on my face. When the parents or children would see that look on my face, maybe it reminded them of their truth as well. Maybe deep down they could see the miracle that they were more than just bodies. Healed and whole. Just as God created them to be for all eternity even after the body is laid aside.

Although I incessantly practiced prayer and sending positive energy to all the suffering children and families, I rarely spoke to or engaged any of them. Mostly, it was just a smile and a knowing. I hoped my smile said, "You are not alone. I am feeling what you are feeling. We will learn to move past the pain together." Except for one day when we had a two-week hospital stay due to the typical complications of cancer treatment for poor Jack. We always had a "go bag" sitting in our closet at home for the occasions when we would need to rush to the hospital. Not knowing how long our stay would be, we packed necessities, but not everything. So, it was common for me to walk down to the first floor of the hospital every couple of days to wash a load of laundry in the hospital laundry room. Although I was grateful for the washing machine and dryer, there was only one of each. So, the availability was hit or miss.

One day, I walked down to the first floor to see if the washing machine and dryer were available. There was already a load in the washing machine and a load in the dryer, so I knew I would need to wait. Just when I was about to leave, a woman entered the room. I could tell she had been crying. We began talking only to find out we were in adjacent rooms on the same floor of the hospital. We each had sons who were undergoing treatment for leukemia, and we were both having a rough stay during this hospital visit. It was more than just chance we ended up in the same room together. We really needed one another in that moment. We held a healing space for one another as we talked about what we were experiencing. We discussed the tremendous sadness we constantly felt with the fear of losing our sons. The conversation was full of raw and visceral emotion, and we listened to one another with love and compassion. There were many "me too" moments in the conversation which made both of us feel less alone. By the end of the conversation, we were both crying and hugging one another. She told me, "**You** are full of such strength." I said, "**We** are full of such strength." I told her I would constantly send light and love to her and her son. She said the same. Then, we parted ways.

We never exchanged names or contact information; we were present for each other in that moment only. I thought that I would see her again in cancer clinic or sometime during the rest of our hospital stay, but I never did. But I never forgot her, and I sent her and her family love and light from Jack's hospital room to her son's hospital room next door during our entire hospital stay. After our hospital stay was over, whenever I thought of her and her son, I would do the same.

After that exchange, I started to pay more attention and began the practice of engaging others (even strangers) if I felt guided to do so. Sometimes, people just need to be heard when they are struggling. You don't have to know all the answers, just listen. And if you can allow yourself to be open enough to hold space, listen empathetically, and give your support, then you can really make a difference in a person's life. Even for just one day.

CHAPTER 19

Finding the Truth in Everything

Jack created this piece of art at school when he was still on cancer treatment. It is one of my favorites and it has been proudly displayed on my refrigerator for some time now.

It speaks loudly of the union, love, and connectedness which assisted him in moving through and past those difficult times. This is what I see when I look at this picture.

In the lower right corner, you see the black darkness. Even though he was experiencing a dark time, he chose to impose white star-like images into the darkness. Rays of sunshine, light, and hope that were right beside him in the midst of troubling times.

But the blackness is only a very small part of the picture. Moving out of the small corner of darkness is a never-ending stream of color moving outwards like rays of sunshine with dancing shapes and figures within these rays. Moving forward, out of the darkness, a myriad of color and vibrance reminding Jack (and all of us) of our truth. This truth has no borders or boundaries. It moves forward happily into infinity.

The different colors represent the unique qualities of not only Jack, but each and every person in this world. Each person may have different talents and divine functions in his or her lifetime; however, we are all joined in unity. In an ever-expanded, connected oneness. And, ultimately, our divine purpose is all the same. To unite and to love others. We all do this in different ways and it appears to take different forms. However, it is all the same.

Continue to love one another, everyone. We are all connected and need to feel that love and connectedness from one another. Separately, we are small, but together, we are powerful and amazing. Together we can heal, together we can be at peace, together we can be filled with happiness. -Facebook post March 10, 2019

While we are having the experience of inhabiting separate bodies on this Earth, we will all experience dark times at one point or another. Even if we are having one of those "easy" lives, we will have to eventually experience the sickness and death of the body. The reason why I loved Jack's art piece mentioned above was because the dark time only occupied a small corner of his piece of paper. "Dark times" are only a small part of our existence in this world, and they usually have a transformative effect on us that we would not have otherwise had. Usually, a positive one if we let go of resistance towards the transformation.

In duality, we have the experience of being in different bodies and having different experiences while on this Earth. We all have different gifts. Some people are good at writing. Some are excellent artists. Some are good at talking to people in a way that gives them peace. The list goes on and on. We all have a myriad of different gifts, and we are supposed to use these gifts in our lifetimes. I believe using the spiritual gifts we have been endowed with creates movement towards a healed Universe.

When we allow our gifts to become our life's purpose, then we are in alignment with our higher purpose in uniting and loving all humanity on the planet. Separately, we may not see how bringing fruition to our gifts can help all of humanity. However, as each person allows this creative process to unfold, the effects of this creative power can "add up" and bring great positive change to the world collectively.

All our different gifts are needed. One spiritual gift is no less important than any other. I believe if we all tap into our creative gifts and use them, that we heal and unify all of humanity. If you have the gift of dance, then dance your heart out. I guarantee it will be a positive experience for you and have an uplifting effect on the people around you. If you have the gift of building, then construct whatever designs set your heart on fire. The people who live in those homes or work in those business offices will feel the aliveness in your work. Whatever your particular spiritual gift happens to be, it will have this positive trickle effect that makes our world a more positive place.

Sometimes, people (including me) are not brave enough to use their spiritual gifts. They worry about their own self-judgments and the judgments of others, "Am I good enough? Can I make enough money to live this way? Will other people in my life approve of my decision to make my creative gift my living/my life purpose?" When we are not using our gifts, we may feel lethargic or stagnant. These feelings usually generate to a general malaise of unhappiness because we are not using the gifts we were meant to use in this lifetime. Even if you are at a point in your life where you cannot quit your job and create art for a living, you can still take baby steps in its general direction. Maybe you work your current job for life expenses, but you also place your art pieces for sale at a local business who sells art. That way, you are still using your gifts. You may even find that as you take these baby steps, new opportunities will come your way to allow for you to use your spiritual gifts even more.

You may be asking, "How do I even know what my spiritual gifts are?" Ask yourself this question, "What do you do in life that gives you joy?" As you begin to answer this question, you may find you have more than one spiritual gift. If so, you should use them all as much as possible. Our spiritual gifts may all be different; however, there isn't one that is any less special than any other. In a dualistic world, every person has different needs along with different perspectives and learning experiences. Therefore, the need for the many different spiritual gifts in order to meet these differing needs and perspectives exists. Each person might respond to healing and learning in different ways, and the different spiritual gifts we all possess can contribute to this healing and learning experience. The worldview you present through your medium of creativity might speak to another individual and present a new way of looking at the world. This shift in perspective for the person experiencing your form of creativity could cause a direct link to healing in their life. That is why it is so important to discover and use your spiritual gifts. Creating from your Source will always bring much needed transformative healing to the world. It is your life's purpose. It is what you are meant to accomplish while in a body. Your purpose is to unite and love others through your creative ideas, actions, thoughts, and awareness. Embrace these gifts and use them.

CHAPTER 20

Letting go of Control and Forgiving the Past

Happy 13th Birthday to Jack today! Flooding in St. Louis caused us to cancel our trip to the City Museum, but we still made the best of it yesterday as we celebrated life in our community. We spent time at the Urbana Farmer's Market, a car show at Parkland College (this boy's face lights up when he sees a muscle car), and Biaggis for dinner.

I am so grateful for this child's bravery and kind spirit. He has been a beacon of light for me. I am so happy for his continued healing from his cancer treatment, and I am amazed to watch his continued growth as a human being. The trials we have had to endure as a family during his cancer treatment were challenging. We were faced with a major decision. Do we harden our hearts and become bitter because of what Jack had to go through? Or do we learn to love? Do we learn to let go and trust the path we are on despite the complete lack of control? Once we were able to let go of that control, once we were able to soften our hearts, that was when the most dramatic healing occurred. Not only for

Jack, but for all of us as a family. There is no good reason for anyone to suffer. However, if we can forgive when we are faced with these challenging situations, then our hearts open. We are even able to experience peace and joy despite what is going on around us.

If there is something in your heart that is holding you back from joy today, please know that you can choose at any time to release it. When you forgive it, it no longer can have any power over you. You will be free. I love you, my friends. May all your hearts be filled with joy today. -Facebook post May 5, 2019

*E*ven before Jack's cancer treatment, I have always had a "controlling" personality. I would often micromanage my children for fear of their safety and not give them the space they needed to grow. I chose a profession in law enforcement where I played an authoritative role in society. And I had "my way" of doing things, even seemingly simple things like how the laundry was done. When I entered a situation where I felt like I had no control, then I would become anxious and upset. When something out of my control happened, I would begin cleaning my house. Sounds crazy, but it made me feel better to have control over the cleanliness of my house. It was therapeutic for me to have control over something in this seemingly crazy life when other areas of my life weren't going "my way."

The reason for this need to control was my need to feel safe. I thought if I could control the things around me, then I would be safe from harm. If I can control my children's environment, then my children will be safe from harm. With Jack's cancer diagnosis came the biggest loss of control I have ever had in my whole life. I was sad and frustrated. Not only could I not keep myself safe, but I failed in keeping Jack safe as well. He was in pain. I was in pain. There was nothing I could do to change the situation. Initially, this loss of control left me depressed and lethargic. The first month was terrible. It took tremendous energy to move my body. Sleep was a luxury I couldn't afford. The thought of eating made me nauseous. Security and safety became a distant memory. I thought I would never feel safe again.

At the beginning of Jack's treatment, my controlling nature went into hyperdrive. If he had to suffer, I would find a way for him to suffer as little as possible. I incessantly asked the doctors and nurses questions. I was always trying to find a better way. I would google the numbers imprinted on his medications to make sure he was given the correct pills from the hospital staff and pharmacy. Any time he was outdoors, I would hover over him like a hawk. I was in a constant state of worry, "If he falls down and cuts himself, he may get a bacterial infection in his blood." I kept him away from all pets for fear he might get scratched. If I could have thought of a constructive way to wrap him in bubble wrap, I probably would have done it.

As Jack's treatment progressed, I began to realize that my controlling nature was making everyone feel less safe. My constant hovering over Jack was making him think that he was always minutes away from dying or becoming hospitalized. I was making him feel more anxious about an already fearful diagnosis. In addition to making him feel less safe, I was exhausting myself by expending all this unnecessary energy. This energy would have been much better spent enacting a positive mindset and environment for my child. Slowly and gradually, I learned to let go of this sense of control. I learned to place trust in the doctors and staff. It was okay for me to ask questions, but it was not okay to badger them. I learned to send love and light to the doctors and pray they would make the best possible decisions regarding Jack's health. I needed to trust the Universe and let go of this fear and anxiety. Placing trust in others was difficult for me, but my controlling attitude was not sustainable, and I needed a change in outlook and perspective if I was going to make it through.

I learned to give Jack more space. When he would fall and hurt himself, I stopped "freaking out." Instead, I would calmly say, "Okay, buddy. Let's go clean it up with antibacterial soap and water." I learned to stop hovering over him while he was playing at the playground. I learned to allow him to be a kid in the moments that he was feeling well enough to just be a kid. As my attitude and perspective changed, so did my actions. As my actions changed, Jack noticed the change and he began to feel safer too.

When I stopped trying to "save" Jack, he grew exponentially. He learned to step outside of his comfort zone and gained confidence in his abilities. I wanted to "save" Jack because I didn't want to see him struggle or suffer any pain. However, when he was allowed to "struggle," he found the inner strength and power to rise up and meet some of these challenges on his own. Allowing him to navigate through minor day to day difficulties gave him an experience for him to grow. My efforts in "saving" Jack just prevented him from necessary growth in his life.

I began to realize how little in life we have control over. How things just happen to people all the time without warning and for no particular reason. Car accidents, sickness, death of a loved one, and losing a job. These events occur in the lives of people all the time. They are upsetting and traumatic, and we have no control over these events when they occur. The only thing we can control is the way we react and respond to these events. I had to learn to retrain my brain. When stressful events would occur, I learned to stop (so I wouldn't automatically react) and take a deep breath.

Sometimes, I would ask for help from Spirit, "Okay. What is the best way to handle this situation? What is the best action for me to take?" If I was successful in remaining calm, the best solutions always seemed to appear before me. Sometimes these solutions presented themselves through other people. The process of learning to let go of control and trust Spirit can be scary, but it is a necessary process for growth in our lives.

On the journey to let go of control, one of the biggest lessons happened for me in the below Facebook post:

> While we were on vacation, we were watching a goofy romcom about good luck and bad luck.
>
> Jack: There is no good luck or bad luck, only duality.
>
> Me: Yes!!!
>
> In a dualistic world, we will all experience good and bad times. But it is important not to personalize it and make it a part of our identity. This can cause a person to carry resentment and bitterness in their hearts. Instead, just view it as part of your story. In a world of duality, we ALL experience both.
>
> If you can't be happy in a life situation you are experiencing, you can choose to surrender to a level of acceptance in the situation (especially if it is something you have no control over). Choosing to be present and just allowing the situation to be as it is. Although you may not be able to be happy during the trying times, acceptance can allow for space around the pain we may be experiencing and give us a reprieve.
>
> Keep moving toward the light of enlightenment, my friends. We are all on this journey together. No one is ever alone. -Facebook post July 4, 2019

In the dualistic Universe, we look on a world with a multitude of possibilities, actions, and solutions. However, in reality, we are always presented with only two choices. We can hold onto the experience and make it a part of our identity in the human body, or we can enjoy (or not enjoy) the situation in the given moment and allow ourselves to move into the next moment with the same non-judgment.

It is easy to start feeling sorry for yourself when bad things happen to you. Trust me, I have been the expert on this in the past. I know how easily I can slip from a moment of happiness to a moment of despair when something "bad" happens. However, if you can learn to not take the experience personally, then you will have much more success in letting go and forgiving those "bad" times.

You may ask, "Some people have perfect lives. Nothing 'bad' ever happens to them. My life has been an unending stream of tragedy. In a dualistic experience, shouldn't we all experience both equally?"

My spiritual path and journey have led me to believe that our bodily experience is one of reincarnation. Therefore, it is very possible to have more "good" times than "bad" times during a life experience (and vice versa). It is something that could be balanced out over several lifetimes. Maybe in one life, you are rich and have all your physical needs met; and, in the next, you are poor and struggle for your physical needs daily. When you remember that each individual on this Earth has these positive and negative experiences in the body, then you can learn not to take it personally when the "bad" experiences happen to you. When you can learn to not take these events personally, then it is easier to release them from your psyche.

When we choose to hold on to these "bad" experiences, we usually hold on to them in our physical bodies. Holding on to this negativity can make us feel tired, lethargic, and can even manifest into disease, sickness, and pain. Remember the story of my enlarged uterus which mirrored the same location and type of pain Jack experienced in his cancer diagnosis? Choosing to not let go of the "bad" experience of watching Jack experience cancer treatment affected my own bodily health. I pulled Jack's cancer story into my body. I allowed it to take residence in my body, and I made Jack's cancer diagnosis a part of my identity. That is why it is vitally important to learn to let go and forgive the "bad" events.

You may think, "But how do I know that I have completely forgiven a 'bad' event and released it from my psyche?"

When I look back on a past event, if I begin to experience the same pain, anxiety, and fear that I experienced while the actual event took place, then I have not forgiven the event. If I can look on a past event, and the negative emotions do not begin to rise, then I know that I have forgiven the event.

131

CHAPTER 21

Seeing the Truth in Everything Around You

A s I began traveling down the winding path of my spiritual journey, I noticed some of my thought processes changing. My perspective and the way I viewed the world changed drastically and for the better. I began to see the symbolism of God's light around me in even the most mundane of my everyday activities. I was comforted by its gentle reminder that I am safe, surrounded with love and peace, and aligned with whatever purpose was given me for the day. I gazed upon the streetlight and saw a light guiding me home. I felt the wind blow and move past and around my body, and I was reminded to allow past thoughts to move through my body instead of holding onto them. I began to realize the earthly elements we experience through our five senses all become a matter of perspective. They become something to be decoded, to look past and through, to see the divine light within every "thing" I experienced.

While driving one day, there was a lawnmower on the side of the road heaving large piles of green grass onto the roadway. My initial response was a negative one. I thought, "Great. That lawnmower is going to throw grass all over my clean car." Then, I stopped. I realized I was forming a negative perception of the mild situation, and it was needless. What if I chose to look at the situation with a new set of lenses? What if I chose to look beyond the experience and see past it to witness the light of my Source which is in everything and every situation? It is the light that is in every seemingly separate entity we encounter. This light binds us and connects us at all times. And we can choose to tap in and connect with that light at any time. I took a deep breath. Then, I watched the lawnmower as it threw the blanket of green grass onto the pavement. I thought, "What a beautiful green blanket to guide me on my way home," as I traveled over the emerald clippings with my vehicle. A green road symbolizing the travels of life and spiritual growth. And how nice that it should appear before me as a guide showing me where to go next on my travels.

There are many lessons in the mundane. We just need to change our past perceptions to an unfolding awareness of the light that guides us in our everyday activities. We are never anywhere by accident. We are always exactly where we are supposed to be. The forgiveness lessons surround us like this blanket of green grass clippings; however, we just need to recognize our former patterns of interpretation regarding the world around us (so we can change them).

When we can switch these mind patterns and see the world through our true eyes, we begin to see clearly. When we can drop the labels and identification we place on objects and situations, then we are free of the emotional attachments we place on these objects and situations. This, in turn, frees the mind to be as it was created by our Source. And we have the freedom to become our true selves. The true selves that we have always been but have forgotten about in this time and place. It is a feeling of indescribable vastness, connectedness, and oneness. And it is a feeling we ALL have the ability to attain. We just need to look within ourselves and choose to do our inner work.

As we forgive, our perceptions will adjust in a positive direction as we release what is no longer needed. As we experience the freedom of our truth and expansion, our life experience becomes lighter, regardless of what appears to be happening around

133

us. We begin to see past the "bad" experiences and witness the truth behind the experience. It is an experience of joy and freedom for all bodies on this Earth to experience when they are ready. When you are ready, ask your spirit guides for help. They have been there all along waiting for you to ask. They sit joyously with you and gently whisper the guidance you need to light your way home.

My son has always loved *The Lego Movie*, so I have watched the movie with him repeatedly. I always begin to cry at the end of the movie because of the truth spoken at the final scene between the hero and the villain. The hero, Emmet, tells the villain, President Business, that he doesn't have to be the bad guy. The "hero" tells the "villain" how wonderful and special he is before extending these same principles to every person in the Universe. He makes the point that every person is equally special and amazing.

The truth and wisdom in this scene are so profound. Sometimes we view ourselves as unworthy of good things or give ourselves the label of "the bad guy." And all we really need is for someone to remind us of our truth. That we are all truly beautiful, wonderful human beings with a purpose given to us by our Source to enact in this dualistic world. The hero, Emmet, doesn't stop there. He continues to tell President Business that he is special, but then extends that invitation to all of humanity. It is as though a spirit guide is working through Emmet to remind everyone of the grandness that lies within them. The truth can be found in children's movies.

I enjoy watching a television show on Netflix called *Travelers*. The premise of the show revolves around a future generation of humans that utilize a time traveling mechanism in order to inhabit human beings in the past. The bodies that the "Travelers" inhabit happen at a time when the soul was leaving the body due to death. The "Travelers" come from the future to the past to attempt to stop an apocalyptic event from occurring on Earth.

One of the "Travelers", Philip, inhabits a body that is addicted to heroin. During the television series, Philip struggles with his inherited heroin addiction while attempting to save the world from future destruction.

The struggle that Philip encounters in this television series relays a message regarding our connectedness to our bodies. Although Philip's soul self from the future never struggled with addiction, he was placed in a body where he learned to experience this struggle. Philip's soul was not addicted to heroin, the body he inhabited was addicted to heroin. Philip's role in this series involved vigilance in remembering his true self rather than this connection with his new body. When he could remember his true soul self, he struggled with the heroin addiction less. When he remembered that he was more than just a body, he knew that addiction could not trap him in a box and make him a prisoner. The body was just a mechanism for fulfilling his life purpose in saving the world. The body was temporarily used for a time until Philip did not need it anymore.

We inhabit bodies on the Earthly plane; however, we are much more than just bodies. We have this bodily experience on Earth in order to fulfill our life purpose given to us by our Source. Our life purpose involves forgiving separateness and moving the world towards a unified wholistic experience. Different people need different teachers due to their varied perspectives. One person may respond better to a certain method or specific type of presentation than another.

Sometimes, we view our bodies as more important than they actually are. We identify with the body as being our true self rather than looking deep within to see our truth or our soul self. When we learn to dive deep within ourselves, then we can overcome whatever appears to be happening in our bodies. When we ask for help from our spirit guides, then they will show us how to identify our soul self. We only need to ask. When we learn to identify with our soul self instead of our body, then anything is possible. Tasks that seemed overwhelming before becoming joyous action. The limitations of the body become less frustrating because you have the realization that you are so much more. The miracle of transforming our perceptions from illusions to truth becomes a possibility. The truth can be found in television shows.

As I was driving home from work one day, I heard a song on the radio entitled *Rainbow* by Kacey Musgraves. In the song, the artist sings about a friend experiencing a metaphorical storm experience in his/her life. The friend is armored for the bad weather (or tough life situation) with a raincoat and umbrella to help protect themselves from the storm. The artist continues to sing about the bad past event being over now, and she continues to sing about the sun shining all around her friend. However, the friend in the song still clings to his or her raincoat and umbrella even though the tough life experience has passed. Instead of being in the present moment of sunny happiness, the friend is reliving the painful past and clinging to the only protection he or she had during that time, the raincoat and umbrella. Despite the good and bad times, the artist concludes the chorus by saying a rainbow was always there with the friend. No matter what appears to be happening to you in your life experience, your Source is always there looking out for you.

When a traumatic experience happens in our lives, it can be difficult to fully release the experience. Sometimes we feel as though we need to maintain protections for ourselves to prevent ourselves from having to experience it ever again. That's when we decide to wear the raincoat as a coat of armor despite the sunny weather outside. We keep ourselves cloaked in the raincoat just in case the storm returns. However, when we do not fully let go of the past and choose to experience the fullness and light in the present moment, then we continue to suffer the effects of the past experience instead of the present moment. If we are suffering in the present moment because we have not forgiven a past event, then we are not in the present moment at all. We are stuck in the past along with the trauma of the past event. We are reliving it repeatedly, maybe hoping for a different outcome this time. In fact, the negative event may present itself in different future forms due to our unwillingness to release it from our psyche in the present moment. The truth can be found in song.

On a beautiful spring day, I walked outside to see a rainbow. The rainbow silhouetted behind a black lamppost and a tree overlaid with pink blossoms in my front yard. The beauty and symbolism washed over me, and I took a picture of the representation and reminder of truth. The rainbow symbolizes the miracle of life. As the colors of the rainbow meld together, they hold together everything that is seemingly separate as a whole unit. The perfect representation of oneness in a dualistic world. A promise of oneness despite the perception of separation in this world. Although our differences in bodies are represented by the different colors in the rainbow, we are all one and our vastness extends across the entire sky.

The lamppost reminded me of one of my favorite books, *The Lion, The Witch, and The Wardrobe* by C.S. Lewis. The lamppost represented the light to guide our way home when we become lost. Sometimes, when we garner truth to the ideas of separation, we forget our spirit self. We forget our light within. The lamppost always stays fixed in place, firmly lit. It waits patiently for us when we are lost. It says, "Look at me. I will show you the way. All is not forgotten. I am here when you are ready to look upon me."

And, at last, the pink blossoms on the tree representing new growth. As we continue our journey vacillating between the rainbow and the lamppost, we are continually growing. The new growth that proceeds from taking this journey is beautiful in every way. The beauty in the blossoms on the tree remind us that the journey is worth taking as the beauty within moves to the surface. The truth can be found outside your front door.

As you move forward on your journey in discovering your true self, you begin to notice the truth in everything around you. You see it in nature, in the people around you, and in the books you read. The truth is everywhere waiting for you to uncover it. The illusions around you have the truth within. When we can alter our sight and switch our perception to one of right mindedness, then we will be able to bask in the truth all around us. It will become easier to release past traumas and negative thoughts because we will see the joy that lies within everything instead.

CHAPTER 22

Believing in Miracles

*W*hile witnessing the pain my son was enduring (along with the lack of explanation or reasons for why it was happening), I found myself living at "rock bottom" quite often. Rock bottom can be a depressing and tough place to be; however, it can also be the catalyst for renewal and an arising of positive change. No one enjoys the feeling of "rock bottom." The heaviness and penetrating pressure of "rock bottom" makes it feel like you are suffocating. However, when we experience "rock bottom," there is a forced surrender that occurs. When things are going well, it can be difficult to surrender the busyness of life to Spirit. It is easy to rationalize, "I know I should surrender to my true being, but maybe tomorrow." It is easy to procrastinate the inner work that necessitates forward movement when life seems to be "going well." When a person experiences "rock bottom," surrender becomes imminent. It is in these moments of complete surrender to Spirit that we often experience miracles.

Miracles are joyous, spirit-filled experiences that we encounter in the realm of our physical being. There is no need for miracles in the realm of heaven; however, in the physical realm of time and space, they are necessary pointers to the truth. Miracles become a reminder of our inner light and point us in the direction of our true purpose. We experienced many miracles as a family when it came to my son's cancer diagnosis.

If you remember, earlier in this book, I discussed the miracle which occurred when many perceived bodies came together with one idea and manifested a change in Jack's cancer diagnosis.

Although the beauty and splendor of miracles are apparent, it can be difficult for a person to share their miracle experiences with others. Miracles often violate the rules and regulations of the physical world, so there is worry of judgment, "Will people think I am crazy if I share this story?" However, you will find if you begin sharing your stories of miracles with others, it will give these people permission to share their own stories of miracles too. The judgment that is feared from telling the story will dissolve and disappear from the person telling the story as another person is receiving the story in a positive way. Other people will realize that miracles are a natural part of the spiritual journey as you find the courage to share your miracle stories with others.

Although it is vulnerable for me to share my miracle stories, I know it will help give others courage to share their miracle stories as well. One of my favorite authors, Brene Brown, tells us that vulnerability is strength. Allowing yourself to be vulnerable with another person is a strength. The courage to share our life experiences gives others the courage to share their own life experiences and be their true selves. That is why I will share more of the miracles I experienced in the story of Jack's cancer diagnosis and treatment. I hope it gives all of you the courage to share your miracles with the world as well.

Early in this process, Jack was in pain and we had no answers from doctors. The weekend before he was diagnosed with cancer was a weekend of pain for our entire family. Jack was in physical pain, we had no answers from doctors, and we were experiencing the pain of watching our child suffer. Overcome with sadness, I slept often during this weekend. Anything for a brief escape from the pain.

During one of my sleeping sessions, I woke up to a voice. My husband's grandmother, Gaga, died six months before Jack's cancer diagnosis, but I was surprised to see her standing next to my bed. I describe this moment as being somewhere in between consciousness. I was not fully awake, but I was not asleep either. Gaga had a close relationship and bond with Jack while she was still on this Earth. I believe she was there to give guidance. Gaga told me, "Wake up. Oh, Kate, Jack has had enough. It is time to take him to the emergency room." The half-dream startled me, but within the next 24 hours, I followed the guidance I was given. Without having the same dream, my husband was feeling the need to take Jack to the emergency room despite a recent trip to the doctor only two days ago. Trusting this inner guidance, we took Jack to the hospital. They found the tumor in his pelvis and sent us to the Children's Hospital in Peoria, Illinois, where they were able to make him more comfortable until we could run more tests and uncover more answers.

I am forever grateful for the above miracle. Since the doctors initially could not find anything wrong with Jack, my husband and I were confused on what action we should take regarding our son's pain. The tumor was wrapped around Jack's spinal cord and it was causing a myriad of other issues in his body. If we had not followed the guidance we received, I often wonder if Jack would still be here with us today or if he would have died from the complications the tumor was causing. Guardian angels can take many forms. I believe Gaga's close relationship with Jack on this Earth caused her to continue to watch over him when her body died. As Gaga's spirit-self, she had a fuller and more complete vision of what was occurring in Jack's body. Her extension of love for Jack caused her to intervene and give a message of guidance in the physical world. We love you, Gaga, and are grateful for your love and guardianship over Jack in this physical world. We know you are still watching over him and all of us, and we are grateful for your presence.

While we are in perceived separate bodies in the dimension of time and space, we are all one in Spirit. Therefore, when we leave our bodies behind in "death," we can choose to move between the spirit world and the physical world to give guidance and love to others. The fact that we are all united in Spirit gives us this undeniable power of connectivity that extends across dimensions. The miracle in this truth can assist a person in the physical world in overcoming the fear of being alone. This truth holds out the miraculous hope that we are united with all the seemingly separate things in the physical world. Loneliness is a lie that would attempt to keep us trapped in a body for all eternity. Despite the perception of being separate in the physical world, our inner light is constantly united with all beings in the Universe. There is no such thing as being alone. Divine unity stretches across this dimension of time and space all the way to Heaven. If we are in the right state of mind, we can even experience Heaven here and now while in a body on this Earth.

The next miracle occurred approximately two weeks after Jack began chemotherapy treatment for his cancer diagnosis. The first month of treatment for leukemia is intense and involves strong, frequent chemotherapy, spinal chemotherapy, and high doses of steroids. Since Jack's cancer diagnosis involved a tumor, the doctors expected the tumor to shrink within two weeks. If the tumor shrinks in this time frame, doctors give a higher chance of survival for the patient. If the tumor does not shrink, then the doctors will quickly resort to a different therapy approach. This therapy approach usually involves radiation and a bone marrow transplant when chemotherapy and the high dose steroids do not appear to be working.

Over the first two weeks of Jack's cancer treatment, Jack's cancer did not go away, and it did not appear to be shrinking. This was closely monitored by almost daily ultrasounds of Jack's tumor site. At the two-week point, Jack's oncologist told us we needed to schedule Jack for another Positron Emission Tomography (PET) scan since it appeared the tumor was not shrinking. After the PET scan, if the tumor was still present, we would need to begin discussing other forms of treatment to save

Jack's life. At the conclusion of this doctor's appointment, we drove home in silence.

When we arrived at home, I retreated to my bedroom and closed the door. I was experiencing a "rock bottom" moment, and I was overwhelmed with the thought of surviving my son. I sat on my bedroom floor, hugging my knees into my chest, and began to pray to Spirit in complete surrender. I asked for courage, I asked for guidance, I asked for strength, but most importantly, I begged for guidance on how to cure Jack. My desperation and complete surrender did not go unanswered. During the prayer, my right hand began to vibrate. It felt like my hand was filled with energy and the connected lifeforce of the Universe. Then, I heard a voice, "Place your hand on Jack's tumor." At this time in my life, it seemed like a long shot. I thought I might be going insane. However, I had nothing to lose. I was desperate to do anything to save my son's life.

I walked downstairs to where my son was sitting on the living room couch. He was watching YouTube videos on his tablet. I asked him if I could watch the videos with him, and I placed my energy-filled hand on his back (in the area of the tumor). My hand was filled with heat and tingled with an energy that I could not explain. As I placed my hand on Jack's back, I could feel the energy penetrating and moving into his body. When the heat and tingling sensation ceased, I removed my hand and continued watching videos with Jack.

The next day, we returned to the hospital for Jack's PET scan. After the PET scan was over, we returned home. The doctor told us she would call us as soon as she received the results. It was an hour and forty-minute drive home. The wait was excruciating. The minutes ticked by like hours and the heaviness was penetrating my chest with the anticipation of the results.

When we pulled into the driveway, my cell phone rang. It was the hospital, so I picked up the phone immediately, and began to walk inside the house. Jack's oncologist told me, "I have great news! The tumor is gone!"

"It's gone?!?" I replied. I think I repeated this over and over again about five or six times during the phone conversation.

"Yes, it is gone. We can resume normal treatment for Jack," the oncologist replied.

The oncologist was in disbelief. I was in disbelief. The ultrasound test the day before the PET scan showed the tumor in place (the same size it had always been). And within that 24-hour period, it disappeared. Immediately, I knew that Spirit was responsible for Jack's healing. In my complete and utter surrender, Spirit was able to work through me to transfer that healing energy to Jack. Spirit was telling Jack (and me), "You are more than just a body. Your true self cannot be sick and cannot die." Jack (in his state of surrender) must have received the message and allowed the healing to take place. In my moment of "rock bottom," a miracle occurred. The tumor disappeared and gave Jack a better chance of survival. The tumor disappeared and gave me a lesson in the importance of surrendering to Spirit and listening to my inner voice. The tumor disappeared and gave the entire family a reason to believe in miracles. In one of our moments of "rock bottom," an important lesson was relayed from the Spirit world to our hearts and minds. A lesson that will never be forgotten.

Not only do miracles occur in the physical world, but they can occur in the dream world as well. The final miracle I would like to share with you occurred at another "rock bottom" moment in Jack's cancer treatment. The first nine months of Jack's cancer treatment were particularly difficult. These nine months were taxing for the heart, body, and soul. During one of the many times we had a "rock bottom" experience during these nine months, Jack had a high fever which was not being reduced with the normal medicines. The doctors were using a chemotherapy on Jack which sometimes caused high fevers in children, and

Jack was having this reaction to the chemotherapy. Not only did Jack have a high fever, but he was having terrible abdominal pain. His only escape was sleep, so he slept often during this part of his cancer treatment. The fever was high enough that he needed to be hospitalized. I remember just sitting on the floor by his hospital bed, holding his hand, and staring at his sleeping face. I sat, squatted down on the floor for hours just watching him. I watched him as though he might disappear if I chose to look away. I wished repeatedly that his pain would be taken away, that his fever would be reduced, that he would be able to leave the hospital and go home.

When my soul could no longer take the pain of watching my son in this state, I retreated to the bathroom (the only place in the hospital where I could maintain any semblance of privacy). I fell on the bathroom floor and sobbed. Not just tears, I sobbed loudly. Tears and snot flowed freely down my face, my body was shaking, and I curled up in a ball on the cold bathroom floor. I thought, "If I cry loud enough, maybe God will hear me. Maybe he will send his angels to comfort and heal my son." I prayed that Jack's pain would be transferred to me instead. I couldn't stand to watch my nine-year-old suffer anymore. I stayed on the floor in this state for thirty minutes. I only moved when my husband knocked on the door to check on me.

My body was heavy with sadness and defeat, but eventually, I peeled myself up off of the chilly bathroom floor of our hospital room. I only had the strength to move myself to the couch (which was my bed for the night). My husband promised to watch over Jack so that I could rest. My internal prayers and dialogue kept begging God to give my son relief until I lost consciousness on the couch.

While I was asleep, the spirit world sent me a dream of comfort. To this day, it makes me cry when I talk about it. In the dream, I was resting in a bedroom of a log cabin. As I walked outside of the bedroom, I looked down at my hands. They were the hands of an old woman. I noticed my hair on either side of my shoulders was long and gray. As I walked into the living room, there was a young boy running towards me. The boy had olive skin, brown eyes, and brown hair and he was yelling, "Nana, Nana." I bent my knees towards the ground and opened my arms wide. The small boy embraced me warmly.

I walked into the kitchen and saw a slim woman with dark hair and dark eyes talking on a cell phone. She was standing by a stove cooking dinner. Aware that I was dreaming, I knew I was here to see Jack. I also had a knowing that this woman was Jack's wife. I asked her, "Where is my son?"

She said, "He's outside," and pointed towards the front door. Then, she continued to talk on her cell phone.

I ran to the front door and opened it. There was an extended front porch the length of the front of the house. It was snowing outside, and there was a man shoveling the snow off the porch. The man was bundled in a winter coat, a hat, gloves, and a scarf. I could only see his face peeking out of all the winter clothing. I stood by the front door looking at the man. He stopped shoveling snow, and he looked at me. The man had a full, brown mustache. At first, I did not recognize him. Then, I noticed the full round face and his brown, almond shaped eyes. In the dream, I thought, "Oh my God. This grown man is my son, Jack." I smiled. I was comforted to witness him as a grown man.

Jack seemed concerned that I was outside in the cold weather. He said, "Mom, go back inside. It's freezing out here and you aren't wearing a coat. You are going to get sick." His voice sounded just like my husband's voice, and I knew for certain that this adult man was indeed my son in a future time.

I closed the door and returned to the kitchen. I asked Jack's wife if she needed any help with dinner. Soon after, Jack, his wife, and my grandson were all seated around the kitchen table. We were eating, telling stories, and laughing. During the entire dream, I remember looking down at my body, and being surprised/confused at the differences in my older body. I remember the happiness and joy that filled the kitchen as we sat eating dinner together.

When I woke up from the dream, I felt at peace. I believe that Spirit sent me this dream to show me that Jack would survive his cancer treatment and lead a happy life. The dream was sent to me to give me peace in a time of "rock bottom." To remind me to "hang in there." To give me hope that there would be a happy ending to Jack's story. I have never had a more realistic dream before or since I had this experience. In fact, this experience feels more like a memory than a dream to me when I recount the events of it. It was as though I was transported through a portal in space to a future time rather than ever having dreamt it. The detail and everything which enveloped the dream was just so REAL.

This was one of the most precious miracles I have ever encountered. It gave me hope that there was a light at the end of this dark tunnel. It gave me gratefulness that Spirit sent me this experience, so I could find the strength to continue to care for my sick son. Often, when Jack was having a "bad day" in cancer treatment, I would look back at this dream and be reminded there would be a bright future ahead for him. This hope brought me through many dark times during his treatment. I am forever grateful for it, and I am not sure if I would have been able to endure some of the pain I witnessed without it.

One more thing about miracles. When you witness a miracle, do not be afraid to acknowledge it. People witness miracles every day. Miracles can rock the face of our earthly existence, and sometimes do not make sense to us on a physical plane. Therefore, sometimes, people fear miracles when they see them. In fact, they fear them to the degree that they would rather explain them away than accept them. People will often choose to find rational explanations for a miraculous event.

If a person says they see an angel, these people might say,

"It was a trick of the light," or, "Maybe you haven't been getting enough sleep, and you just THOUGHT you saw an angel."

If a person witnesses a blind man cured of his inability to see, they might say, "Was he ever blind to begin with? There has to be some medical explanation to explain this."

Why do we sometimes choose to explain away the most amazing events that occur in our lives? Why are we so afraid of them? There is always another choice to be made. One that will make you much happier. When you witness a miracle, acknowledge it, let it be, and allow the miracle to transform you. Choosing to view the miracle in this way will be life changing for you. Not only will the miracle change your life, but it will extend out and move the lives of others in a positive direction as you share it with them. Don't be afraid of miracles. Witness it, bask in its splendor, and rejoice!

CHAPTER 23

Pain is all the Same

O n January 2, 2020, I woke up bright and early. Ready to
start the New Year right. I drove to my fitness center and
hopped on the Peloton bike with the goal of staying physically
healthy this year. As I rode the bike, huffing, puffing, panting
(and wondering what in the hell I was thinking, the Peloton bike
workouts are hard!), I listened to the words of the instructor
on the television screen in front of me. At the beginning of the
workout, this instructor usually gives a preview of the entire
workout so you can mentally prepare for what is ahead. But,
today, she said, "I'm not going to give you a preview today. I want
you to be in the present moment as it is happening."

"Oh no," I thought, "How will I make it through this tough
workout when I don't know when the hard parts are coming
up?" Then, I remembered, in life, we usually don't receive any fair
warning when the "hard parts" are about to happen. The tough
times just happen, and we are left with the present moment to
help guide us through them. We bring our perceptions and grace
to the present moment with the knowledge our union with a
Higher Power will gently assist us through and past the "hard
part." No wonder she is my favorite Peloton instructor. Thank
you, Tunde!

So, I began my Peloton ride with the confidence that I will
move through the "hard parts" with self-love, non-judgment,
and plenty of sweat dripping off my face. Approximately ten
minutes into the workout, the Peloton instructor was welcoming
the year 2020, and she was reflecting on the past decade. She

dedicated this 30-minute workout to her favorite music in the past decade, and she began to discuss the memories she had associated with some of this music. She talked about how her nineteen-year-old brother died in this decade. Three years later, her father died. Three years after that, her mother died. Not only was sweat streaming down my cheeks, but my eyes began to glass over as I listened to her words. She continued to say how she lives her life in honor of them. She did not complain that she had just experienced a difficult decade in her life. She did not blame anyone for her loss. She stayed in the present moment and kept moving on her bike. She did this to honor her family and to live her life joyously in their absence.

And it dawned on me, that everyone on this Earth suffers from some form of trauma. It doesn't matter what form it takes; it is all the same. A break-up in a relationship, the death of a loved one, losing a job, physical abuse, mental abuse, etc. It all makes the human body feel the same. The heaviness in the chest, the depression, the sinking feeling in the stomach, and the numbness in the body. Whatever form the painful experience may take, the physical expression in the human body is similar for each and every human being.

Sometimes, we want to identify with our pain and compare it to the pain of others. It becomes a competition, "My pain is worse than your pain." Our society would tell us that some forms of pain are worse than others. Society may say the physical harm of a child is worse than the physical harm of an adult. Or, a divorce after twenty years of marriage causes worse pain than a teenage break up with a boyfriend or girlfriend. I disagree. The pain manifests itself in similar patterns in the body (physically and emotionally) regardless of the event which caused the pain. Regardless of the form, all pain is the same.

When we realize this, then we can begin to empathize and show greater compassion for the pain that others are experiencing. Rather than attempting to compete for who has experienced the worst pain and making our pain a permanent part of our bodily existence (a part of our identity), we discover the similarities in the different forms of pain our outer world presents. Often, pain will cause fear, anxiety, or despair. When we stop attempting to define different forms of pain but recognize that pain manifests itself in the same physical and emotional forms in the physical body, then we can learn to come together and uncover solutions towards healing.

Maybe we realize that our collective pain is a part of a larger spiritual process. Perhaps, the pain is pointing a finger in the direction of where we should travel next on our spiritual journey. As I have studied *A Course in Miracles*, I have learned that pain is a form of unconscious guilt. We experience this pain in different forms; however, it stems from our seemingly separate lives away from God as we live our lives in bodies in a dualistic world. Of course, we could never really be separated by the Spirit that created us. We are always connected to our Source. In bodies, we just have an awareness that we are separated from our Source (which causes the unconscious guilt). So, the pain may take different forms in the dualistic world; however, it has the same root cause (the unconscious guilt due to our seemingly separation from God).

As we uncover the true reason for the pain (when we can name it), then we become less afraid of it. We can begin to work together to release the unconscious guilt which masquerades itself in different forms in the physical world. We learn to identify less with our pain and more with our truth and light.

My Peloton bike ride was a wonderful reminder. Every person around us has experienced a form of trauma in their lifetime. Instead of feeling sorry for one another, we can unite and support one another on our journeys instead. Instead of ignoring or trying to eliminate the pain, we can name it, surrender to it, and allow it to dissolve on its own (with assistance from Spirit). We can work to build one another up and release the suffering we do not need in our lives anymore. We are not alone in our pain, we are surrounded by others (with different experiences), but the same painful feelings. Therefore, we do not need to personalize our pain, compare it to the pain of others, or make pain a part of our identity. Instead, we learn to surrender to the pain, let it change and transform us, and move us in the direction we need to go. And since pain is something we all experience, we don't have to travel this journey alone. We can do it hand in hand. We can do it together.

CHAPTER 24

Feeling Alone? You are Enough.

Sometimes we feel like uniting with others in order to move past our tough times. However, there are other times when we feel alone in our difficult situations or we feel like there is no one who can relate to us. We may feel like we have no one to discuss our feelings with. And there are certainly times when we may not have someone to assist us in moving through the tough terrain of our life journey. Our tiresome paths may have us feeling helpless and alone. I have experienced this feeling several times in my lifetime. When I asked how to move through it in a meditation, I was given the following vision:

> There was a young woman with long, black hair standing outside in a tropical jungle. She wore no clothing, and her long, black hair covered most of the top half of her body like a shawl. She was tired of the world around her, and she was walking towards a large temple. She was seeking for answers to her spiritual truth. As she walked towards the temple, she was filled with fearful thoughts, "What if I am sacrificed? What if I am not ready to confront the truth? What if I am not accepted in this place? What if I am not ready?"
> There were at least 100 steps which led to the entrance of the massive temple. As she rose up the steps, one by one, more uncertainty entered her mind, "Who will greet me in this temple? Will

153

there be Gods to greet me? Angels? Who will be my guide in this place?" Yet, she kept walking forward, knowing it was time to find the answers to these questions. Knowing there was no turning back. She had looked for these answers in many places in the world only to become frustrated and confused.

As she entered the door of the temple, she expected to be greeted by a council who might judge her severely. She expected to be surrounded by many spirits. She expected to enter a room filled with extravagant furniture and decoration. But as she bravely entered the temple and peered around the room, she witnessed none of these things. She saw a large hearth with a blazing fire in front of her. She looked to her left and to her right expecting to find more surrounding her. She wondered, "Am I missing something?" There was nothing else in the room except herself and the fire. She was confused, "How can it be I came here looking for answers, but find myself alone? Will no one be my guide? Am I a lost cause?"

Then, it dawned on her. The fire represented her power, strength, and light. She was one with the fire and it represented her own true spirit. Her initial loneliness in that moment reminded her of her true light and power. The room was not empty because she was not ready for the truth. The room was empty because the truth was already inside her. In that moment, she realized she didn't need anything or anyone else in order to reach enlightenment. The truth was within her all along. She only needed to look within for these answers. And, now, she did not feel alone. She felt the largeness and expansion of her true awareness. She laughed out loud in the temple and the sound echoed all around her. The truth was within her. She did not have to look to the outside world for answers. She was enough. She peered within and found the answers to her very being. She became enlightened and could now move about the Earth free of the nagging questions that formerly plagued her. She was free.

There are times in our life when we find ourselves surrounded by friends, family, and community support. Then, there are times when you are devoid of all three. During the times when you feel the most alone, it is important to know that you are enough. God's creative light and essence is at the heart of every living (and seemingly non-living) thing in this world. This means this light and power is within you waiting patiently for you to uncover it.

In the chaos of life, we forget our truth. We forget the light of God is lying dormant within us. We cover our light with politics, work, television, false truths, plastic surgery, exercise, video games, etc. Not that any of these things are bad in and of themselves. But when we are primarily focused on everything outside of us, then we forget about what is lying dormant inside of us. We are distracting ourselves from our true light within by keeping our focus on the busyness of the world instead. We are choosing the outside world distractions over our ultimate peace and happiness.

When we can learn to make space for ourselves in order to still the mind (through walks in nature, meditation, prayer, etc.), we begin to be reminded of that light and power within ourselves. When we remember the light and power given to us by our Source, we realize that we are truly limitless. We don't have to look to the outside world to fulfill our needs. All our needs are already met within. God gave us everything we need within ourselves to be happy and at peace at all times. We only need to surrender to Spirit and allow it to come forth. We need to believe in our inner light and power so we can strengthen and empower it further. So that the dim forgotten light can reignite and become the roaring fire in the hearth of the temple. Yes, YOU are that powerful.

Jesus says in *The Holy Bible*, New King James Version in John 8:12, "I am the Light of the World." But what we have forgotten is that God placed the same light he placed into Jesus into every one of us as well. God is within you. And if Source is within you, then you are the most joyous, peaceful, happy being. You are united with God and that same light is within all the other bodies surrounding you. You only need to ask Spirit for assistance, trust that you are walking on the right path, and be determined to find the courage to look within. Learn to believe in yourself. You don't need the outside world to fulfill you, you are already fulfilled. The outside world can be as it is, and you can be united with your light and allow the worries the world possesses to melt away. You don't need anything else, but that light within you. Don't be afraid to unite with it. YOU ARE ENOUGH.

A FINAL NOTE

*A*s of February 2020, Jack is 1 ½ years past cancer treatment and he is still cancer free. His body, mind, and spirit continue to heal as a process from the chemotherapy and stress presented to his psyche. However, he is currently living his life much like other thirteen-year-old boys. My mind, body, and spirit continue to heal from the event as well. The journey to healing is not easy. We continue to heal together and support one another in the healing process. This includes being patient with one another and trusting Spirit in the moments where we appear to lose ourselves completely. The journey to healing may be long, but it is certainly one worth taking. May your journey to healing be a prosperous one.

Printed in the United States
by Bookmasters

Printed in the United States
By Bookmasters